# The PARABLES of *Jesus*

## CLARENCE SEXTON

# CROWN
## PUBLICATIONS
*Royal Reading*

# The
# PARABLES
## of
# Jesus

## CLARENCE SEXTON

FIRST EDITION
COPYRIGHT
OCTOBER 2002

CROWN
PUBLICATIONS
*Royal Reading*

1700 BEAVER CREEK DRIVE
POWELL, TENNESSEE ❖ 37849
1-877 AT CROWN
www.FaithfortheFamily.com

## THE PARABLES OF JESUS

Copyright © 2002

Crown Publications

Powell, Tennessee 37849

ISBN: 1-58981-118-6

Layout and design by Stephen Troell

Printed in the United States of America

# Dedication

This book is affectionately dedicated to Dr. Tom Sexton. God gave me one brother who is thirteen months younger than I am. He carries our father's name, Preston Thomas Sexton. He is a faithful preacher and is being mightily used of God. As I think about the greatest stories ever told, I think about the amazing grace of God in my brother's life. I love him dearly. He is my friend and encourager.

*Clarence Sexton*

*Acts 5:42*

# Introduction

According to II Timothy 3:15-16, the work of the Word of God is to make us wise unto salvation, to teach us doctrine, to reprove us, to correct us, and to instruct us in righteousness. It is my prayer that this book on the parables of Jesus, the greatest stories ever told, will be mightily used of God in your life.

Yours in Christ,

*Clarence Sexton*

*Acts 5:42*

# Contents

# Chapter One

# THE HEARERS
# AND THE DOERS

 early one third of the recorded teachings of Jesus Christ are given to us in parables. We must understand the parables of Christ to understand the teaching of Christ. All of His parables are found in the first three Gospel records: the Gospel according to Matthew, the Gospel according to Mark, and the Gospel according to Luke.

Parables are not fables, for parables come from real situations. The word *parable* means "to cast alongside." It is a story cast alongside a spiritual truth to help us understand the spiritual truth. Parables are not allegories. An allegory has some meaning in practically every detail. A parable is not interpreted that way. A parable is a story given by the Lord Jesus Christ with one great truth or great lesson for us. As we study these parables given by the Lord Jesus, we will see that these are the greatest stories ever told.

The Bible says in Matthew 7:24-29,

> *Therefore whosoever heareth these sayings of mine, and doeth them, I will liken him unto a wise man, which built his house upon a rock: and the rain descended, and the floods came, and the winds blew, and beat upon that house; and it fell not: for it was founded upon a rock. And every one that heareth these sayings of mine, and doeth them not, shall be likened unto a foolish man, which built his house upon the sand: and the rain descended, and the floods came, and the winds blew, and beat upon that house; and it fell: and great was the fall of it. And it came to pass, when Jesus had ended these sayings, the people were astonished at his doctrine: for he taught them as one having authority, and not as the scribes.*

There are those who hear and do and those who hear and do not do. Let us consider the hearers and the doers.

In this parable given by the Lord Jesus, we find that all people build. They do not all build on the same foundation, but they all build. There are no gray areas here. The Lord Jesus speaks with finality. Notice what He says in the twenty-third verse, *"And then will I profess unto them, I never knew you."*

He does not say, "I knew you occasionally," or "I once knew you." He says, *"I never knew you."* The parable in the very next verse relates to this passage because the verse begins with the word, *"therefore."*

In Matthew 7:21-22 the Bible says,

> *Not every one that saith unto me, Lord, Lord, shall enter into the kingdom of heaven; but he that doeth the will of my Father which is in heaven. Many will say to me in that day, Lord, Lord, have we not prophesied in*

*thy name? and in thy name have cast out devils? and
in thy name done many wonderful works?*

They said, *"We have done many wonderful works."* They were
doers, but it does not make any difference what you have done if
what you have done is not on the right foundation.

All people are building some kind of life, but we must give earnest
heed to the right foundation. There are people who are active in
providing things for the needy. No doubt
these people have the idea that they are
pleasing God by their benevolent deeds.
Even people in good churches get the idea
that just because they are busy doing good
things they are making the Lord happy.
But we must consider the foundation.

> *All people are
> building some
> kind of life, but
> we must give
> earnest heed to
> the right
> foundation.*

In this parable the same rain, the same
flood, the same torrential storm came to
both builders. Some people have the idea
that, because they are Christians, they are
going to escape the storms. The fact that
you are a Christian does not mean you are going to escape the storm,
but it does mean you have a refuge. According to this parable, the
refuge is in the foundation. If your life is built on the Lord Jesus
Christ, when the rain comes then your "house on the Rock" will
stand firm. The foundation is sure.

Both houses looked safe, but both were not safe. One house
appeared to be safe, but it was built on the wrong foundation. The
emphasis was not on the material that was used for the structure, but
on the foundation.

There are people who do "religious" things, but they do not please
God with those things. Others do things in the church, and they
please the Lord. Why? Are you busy for the Lord because of what

He has done for you? Or are you busy for Him in order to get something from Him, even His approval?

All religions basically fall into two categories. One says that Jesus Christ has finished the perfect work of salvation on the cross. It is done, and all we must do is repent and believe. In all other religions, people are constantly doing things to please God and get to God. This is salvation by works. We should work, but we work because we are saved, not in order to get saved.

Looking at this entire passage of Scripture in the larger context, we find what is referred to as the Sermon on the Mount. It begins with the Beatitudes and concludes with a very severe warning. When the Lord concluded this particular time of teaching, He gave this story about the builders.

## THE PERSON SPEAKING

The Bible says in Matthew 7:28-29, *"And it came to pass, when Jesus had ended these sayings, the people were astonished at his doctrine: for he taught them as one having authority, and not as the scribes."*

Christ spoke with authority. When people heard Him speak, there was no misunderstanding of His words. They knew what He had said when He had finished. He drew the line. There have always been people who wanted to use the idea of tolerance to excuse an unwillingness to draw the line. This is not the way the Lord Jesus taught.

In this age in which we live, we hear much of tolerance. This is really a term for religious compromise. Many people applaud this idea of tolerating everything. We are living in a day when evil is called good, and good is called evil. Right is called wrong, and wrong is called right. We need to decide as God's children that we are not going to be ashamed to declare what we believe.

Some people want to take all the "bite" out of teaching and preaching. They want to make it soothing, smooth, and delightfully interesting. Preachers are out; ministers are in. Sermons are out; talks are in.

The Bible says that the Lord spoke as *"one having authority."* He is God incarnate, robed in flesh. He spoke God's Word. When men stand to speak the oracles of God, to hold God's Word in their hands, to declare the Word of God to the people, they speak with authority. The person speaking in this parable is none other than God Himself. We need to give heed to what He says.

In this parable, the Lord Jesus makes great distinction between those who hear and do not do, and those who hear and do.

The Bible says in Luke 6:45-46, *"A good man out of the good treasure of his heart bringeth forth that which is good; and an evil man out of the evil treasure of his heart bringeth forth that which is evil: for of the abundance of the heart his mouth speaketh. And why call ye me, Lord, Lord, and do not the things which I say?"*

> *The fact that you are a Christian does not mean you are going to escape the storm, but it does mean you have a refuge.*

It is hypocritical on our part to condemn the people in Christ's day who listened and did not obey when we have His Word to hear and we do not obey. It is always easy to condemn other people. It is easy to find the man who is doing things we do not do, and talk about how evil and awful he is. Jesus Christ, God Almighty, is speaking. This thought should stir our hearts and arouse our attention.

# THE PRINCIPLE STATED

The Lord draws this particular session to a conclusion as He says in Matthew 7:24, *"Therefore whosoever heareth these sayings of mine..."*

Some believe that the only thing we should heed in the Bible is the Sermon on the Mount; in reality, we should condense the Bible to *"these sayings."*

Christ gives a principle here about a foundation, and He says that the way to get the foundation is to hear and heed. Some people build on the Rock. The Rock, of course, is a type of the Lord Jesus. Some people build on the sand. What does this mean? If I say, "We need to build our lives on the Lord; He is the only foundation," what does that mean? If we say, "Don't build your life on the sand; it is sinking sand," what does that mean?

*Christ spoke with authority. When people heard Him speak, there was no misunderstanding of His words.*

The apostle Paul wrote about the foundation of the church in Corinth. In I Corinthians 3:11-13 he declares,

*For other foundation can no man lay than that is laid, which is Jesus Christ. Now if any man build upon this foundation gold, silver, precious stones, wood, hay, stubble; every man's work shall be made manifest: for the day shall declare it, because it shall be revealed by fire; and the fire shall try every man's work of what sort it is.*

This particular passage is dealing with the judgment seat of Christ and our work as Christians. The idea in verse eleven is that the only foundation on which we can build our lives is Jesus Christ. What does it mean to say, "Build your life on Jesus Christ"? To build your life on Jesus Christ means that you believe that what He says is final, what He says is forever, what He says never changes, and what He says is always true. Building your life on Christ is taking Him at His Word, and no matter what the world is saying, building your life on the Word of God. The only sure foundation is Jesus Christ. Heaven and earth will pass away, but His Word will stand forever. We must build on the Rock; this Rock is the Lord Jesus.

In every generation people are looking for new ideas. To give you an example, we can look at education in our country. The last generation of young people coming through American educational institutions was taught to read with a so-called "principle" which their teachers found did not work. Educators also experimented with math and tried to teach a generation of young people in our public education system a new way of doing math. They declared later, after that generation was wasted in the experiment, that it did not work.

> *The only sure foundation is Jesus Christ.*

Our Christian lives do not have to be experiments. We do not have to grab hold of some new idea, some enlarged revelation, something that people want to add to the Bible. We do not have to go beyond the Bible for anything. Christ is all-sufficient; His Word is all-sufficient. In any generation, even in this so-called "enlightened" generation in which we live, when something does not line up with the Bible, it is sand, not stone. The principle is to build your life on the Rock. The Rock is Jesus Christ.

How do we do this? We build by hearing and doing. This is the principle. It is a foolish thing for us to know that God is speaking to our hearts, yet make no response to what the Lord is saying. I heard a preacher say years ago that, when the Spirit of God deals with us, we should be obedient to Him immediately. Delay is disobedience.

A former pastor of mine said, "When you are in a meeting where God's Word has gone forth and the Spirit of God is dealing with you, imagine that Jesus Christ is standing at the end of the aisle with an open hand saying, 'Come to me.'" The Holy Spirit is just as much God as God the Son. When the Holy Spirit speaks to us, convicts us, and draws us to Himself, we should be as obedient to the Holy Spirit in that moment as we would be if we could see Jesus Christ standing at the end of the aisle inviting us to come to Him.

Of course, there are times when God deals with us outside the church services. Whenever He speaks, we should obey. Obedience is not simply doing His will; it is delighting in doing His will. Where do these impressions come from that deal with us about doing right things–calling someone, writing someone, giving some instruction about Christ, or telling others of Him? The Holy Spirit, who lives in us, gives us these impressions as we walk with Him during the day. We should be obedient. The principle in this parable is to hear and to obey.

## THE PROMISE MADE

I love the promise made in this passage. It is very simple but profound. The Bible says in Matthew 7:24-25,

> *Therefore whosoever heareth these sayings of mine, and doeth them, I will liken him unto a wise man, which built his house upon a rock: and the rain descended, and the floods came, and the winds blew, and beat upon that house; and it fell not: for it was founded upon a rock.*

This is the promise, *"It fell not."* You may say, "How important is that?" It is very important. Look at the other side of this story in verses twenty-six and twenty-seven,

> *And every one that heareth these sayings of mine, and doeth them not, shall be likened unto a foolish*

*man, which built his house upon the sand: and the rain descended, and the floods came, and the winds blew, and beat upon that house; and it fell: and great was the fall of it.*

Sometimes in our eagerness to give good counsel, we hurt people. We tell people, "Come to church. Get in Sunday School. Join the choir. Get involved. Do something." We put the cart before the horse. We need to say, "How is your relationship and fellowship with Jesus Christ? Do you believe it would please the Lord Jesus for you to be in church faithfully? Do you believe it would please the Lord Jesus for you to serve Him?"

Why should we serve the Lord? There are some verses in Ephesians chapter two that help explain this. We often quote verses eight and nine of this chapter, *"For by grace are ye saved through faith; and that not of yourselves: it is the gift of God: not of works, lest any man should boast."*

> *It is a foolish thing for us to know that God is speaking to our hearts, yet make no response to what the Lord is saying.*

These are beautiful verses, and we need to know that we are not saved by works, but the Bible says in verse ten, *"For we are his workmanship, created in Christ Jesus unto good works, which God hath before ordained that we should walk in them."*

We do not work to get saved; we work and serve the Lord because we are saved. As we hear, obey, and build on the foundation of our salvation, the Bible says we are not going to fall. There is much stumbling in life. There is much slipping, and we get off track sometimes, but God says we are not going to fall. He is going to keep us saved. He is going to bring us into our *"desired haven"* as we hear and obey.

Apply this to your daily life, and it becomes more personal. Maybe one of your children or someone you are trying to help says, "I need money." Good! If you have money to give, give it. Give him the coat off your back, but ask him, "Do you know the Lord? Have you trusted Christ as your Savior?" If he says, "Yes," then say, "Let me ask you this. What is it God wants you to do?" If he is not willing to do what God desires, you can try to help him all you want, but he is going to keep falling, and falling, and falling.

> *As we hear, obey, and build on the foundation of our salvation, the Bible says we are not going to fall.*

Sometimes there are people in families who get irritated with one another. Friends and neighbors get irritated with one another. They say, "You won't help me." We say sometimes, "You need to help yourself." What we really mean by this is, "You need to obey God for yourself."

A person can be bailed out a hundred times, but until he is willing to trust Christ as Savior and obey Christ, he is never going to be on the Rock. He is going to build on the sand, and he is going to fall. We often see this in life, and the fall is heart-wrenching.

The storms are coming. They come to all people. The promise is that those on the Rock will not fall. He said that, when the storm came, the house on the Rock *"fell not."*

Be a hearer and a doer of the Word of God. Some things seem impossible to accomplish. We need to realize that it is not up to us to do it; it is up to us to obey the Lord, and He will do it. Ours is the work of obeying. His work is the work of bringing it to pass.

I hear people say all the time, "Preacher, I can't. I just can't." You do not have to. You just have to say, "I am going to take the first step of obedience," and you will see God come through and do some things that only He can do. We must begin to obey.

Each one of us is standing in front of something at this moment that demands a step of faith to be obedient to God and please Him. May God help us to take that step by faith.

# THE SOWER

n Matthew 13:1-9 our Lord gives us the parable of the sower. He then explains the parable in verses eighteen through twenty-three. In the eighteenth verse He calls this, *"the parable of the sower."*

This particular parable of the sower is very important. Speaking of this parable Mark 4:13 says, *"And he said unto them, Know ye not this parable? and how then will ye know all parables?"*

Jesus Christ not only gave the parable, He interpreted the parable so there is no way we can miss what it means. As we look again in the thirteenth chapter of the Gospel according to Matthew, the Bible says in verse thirty-five, *"That it might be fulfilled which was spoken by the prophet, saying, I will open my mouth in parables; I will utter things which have been kept secret from the foundation of the world."*

Christ quotes here from Psalm 78:2 which says, *"I will open my mouth in a parable: I will utter dark sayings of old."*

He reveals to us, especially in these seven parables given in Matthew thirteen, the mysteries of the kingdom or the rule of the Lord. The first four parables are spoken to the multitude in general. The last three of these parables are spoken to Christ's disciples. The first of these mystery parables is *"the parable of the sower."*

The Bible says in Matthew 13:1, *"The same day went Jesus out of the house, and sat by the sea side."* The setting for this parable is along the Sea of Galilee, no doubt near the city of Capernaum. As the Lord Jesus stepped out of a house, He began to speak with parabolic teachings. The Word of God says in Matthew 13:2-9,

> *And great multitudes were gathered together unto him, so that he went into a ship, and sat; and the whole multitude stood on the shore. And he spake many things unto them in parables, saying, Behold, a sower went forth to sow; and when he sowed, some seeds fell by the way side, and the fowls came and devoured them up: some fell upon stony places, where they had not much earth: and forthwith they sprung up, because they had no deepness of earth: and when the sun was up, they were scorched; and because they had no root, they withered away. And some fell among thorns; and the thorns sprung up, and choked them: but other fell into good ground, and brought forth fruit, some an hundredfold, some sixtyfold, some thirtyfold. Who hath ears to hear, let him hear.*

Notice the expression, *"let him hear."* Many times when the Word of God is spoken, we place the emphasis on the speaker; here, the Lord Jesus Christ places the emphasis on the hearer.

Did you ever wonder what happens to the Word of God and all the preaching and teaching of the Word of God that goes forth? Our Lord came on the scene and said, "Let us place the emphasis on the hearer." In particular, He spoke about the soil of the human heart. Of course, His inquiring disciples asked Him why He spoke in parables. He quoted a passage from the book of Isaiah. Notice Matthew 13:15,

> *For this people's heart is waxed gross, and their ears are dull of hearing, and their eyes they have closed; lest at any time they should see with their eyes, and hear with their ears, and should understand with their heart, and should be converted, and I should heal them.*

The Lord Jesus gave these stories, which we shall call "the greatest stories ever told," to arouse the interest and curiosity of these people. As I stated earlier, if you consider all the recorded teachings of Jesus Christ, one third of what He taught is given to us in parables. Surely the Lord wants us to understand these parables so we can understand His teachings.

Let us look at the interpretation for a moment. The Bible says in Matthew 13:18-23,

> *Hear ye therefore the parable of the sower. When any one heareth the word of the kingdom, and understandeth it not, then cometh the wicked one, and catcheth away that which was sown in his heart. This is he which received seed by the way side. But he that received the seed into stony places, the same is he that heareth the word, and anon with joy receiveth it; yet hath he not root in himself, but dureth for a while: for when tribulation or persecution ariseth because of the word, by and by he is offended. He also that received seed among the thorns is he that heareth the word; and the care of this world, and the deceitfulness of*

*riches, choke the word, and he becometh unfruitful. But he that received seed into the good ground is he that heareth the word, and understandeth it; which also beareth fruit, and bringeth forth, some an hundredfold, some sixty, some thirty.*

I am a Christian because I heard the Word of God and received it. If you are saved, if you have been born again, if you have asked God to forgive your sin and by faith received Jesus Christ as your Savior, it is because you heard and received the Word of God. Those who have been born into God's family were born by the Word of God. We are saved by hearing, believing, and receiving God's Word.

> *Those who have been born into God's family were born by the Word of God.*

For any progress or development in my Christian life that might be called Christlikeness, I must thank God for His working in my heart so that I could receive His clear teaching. The clear teaching of the Word of God has produced fruit in my life.

As far as my testimony is concerned, I may say to you that I asked God to forgive my sin and by faith received Jesus Christ as my personal Savior after hearing and receiving the Word of God. However, I prove that I am a Christian, not by giving my testimony but by the fact that there is fruit in my life produced by the Word of God.

Some people say that they have received Christ as their Savior; they give a clear testimony about a time when they asked God to forgive their sin and by faith received the Lord as their Savior. They give their testimony, but there is no real evidence in their daily lives that they are Christians because there is no fruit produced by the Word of God.

Forty-eight times in Matthew, Mark, and Luke, the word *parable* is used. As we look at the parables, remember that we are primarily looking for one great truth in each of the parables. We may give consideration to other things, but what one great truth is the Lord Jesus driving home to our hearts?

I think you will see, after looking at this particular parable, that we must examine our hearts to see what the soil of our lives is really like. There is no problem with the sower. There is no problem with the seed. The problem is with the soil.

# THE SEED

In I Peter 1:18-23 the Bible says,

> *Forasmuch as ye know that ye were not redeemed with corruptible things, as silver and gold, from your vain conversation received by tradition from your fathers; but with the precious blood of Christ as of a lamb without blemish and without spot: who verily was foreordained before the foundation of the world, but was manifest in these last times for you, who by him do believe in God, that raised him up from the dead, and gave him glory; that your faith and hope might be in God. Seeing ye have purified your souls in obeying the truth through the Spirit unto unfeigned love of the brethren, see that ye love one another with a pure heart fervently: being born again, not of corruptible seed, but of incorruptible, by the word of God, which liveth and abideth for ever.*

When Jesus Christ spoke that day by the seaside in Galilee, the words that came from His mouth were not corruptible words; they were incorruptible words. It was seed *"which liveth and abideth for ever."* When we hold the Bible in our hands and give forth the Word of God, we are giving the same incorruptible seed that Christ gave that day in Galilee.

It is living seed. It is life-changing seed. It is fruit-producing seed. May God help us to see again the power of the seed. May we be people who preach, teach, and give out the Word of God. No wonder the Lord says that God's Word *"shall not return unto me void"* (Isaiah 55:11). The Word of God lives and abides forever. It is the seed.

# THE SOWER

In this parable, Jesus Christ is sowing the seed. He is giving the Word of God. We can all enter into partnership with God by sowing the seed.

In Psalm 126:1-6 the Bible says,

> *When the LORD turned again the captivity of Zion, we were like them that dream. Then was our mouth filled with laughter, and our tongue with singing: then said they among the heathen, The LORD hath done great things for them. The LORD hath done great things for us; whereof we are glad. Turn again our captivity, O LORD, as the streams in the south. They that sow in tears shall reap in joy. He that goeth forth and weepeth, bearing precious seed, shall doubtless come again with rejoicing, bringing his sheaves with him.*

The Bible speaks here of sowing in tears. All of us should sow. We sow the Word of God by preaching it, teaching it, giving out gospel tracts, telling people the Word of God, and quoting Bible verses. By giving God's message to a lost and dying world, we are sowers of the seed.

# THE SOIL

Too often we want to be soil samplers before we sow the seed. We should not do this. We should not inspect the soil to see if we think the soil will take the seed. We should simply sow the seed and leave the rest in God's hands.

Do not take this parable and attempt to prove that only twenty-five percent of the people you speak to about Christ will believe the gospel. I do not believe we can put percentages on this, but we do see different types of hearts in this parable.

*We must examine our hearts to see what the soil of our lives is really like.*

If we had followed the Lord Jesus Christ during His earthly ministry, we would have found all these kinds of people around the Lord. There were people who had absolutely no interest at all in what He was saying, while others had only a casual interest. They looked quickly, but their casual interest was soon gone. We would have found people who seemed to be sincere followers, who professed to believe and receive, but when things got tough and Christ's words were strong, they turned back and followed Him no more.

Of course, some had good ground in their hearts. That does not mean they were good because there is *"none righteous, no, not one"* (Romans 3:10). However, they had hearts that received seed. They came to know the Lord as their Savior and became fruit-bearing Christians. What kind of heart do you have?

In application, let us take this a step further. We must keep the soil as good as we can. Our hearts can grow hardened, and our lives can become fruitless even after we have trusted the Lord as our personal Savior. You may attend church faithfully but have allowed things in the eye-gate or ear-gate that never should have been allowed. This has badly affected the soil of your heart.

Perhaps there was a time when you gladly received God's Word; you were hungry and thirsty to hear from the Lord. You were like fertile soil waiting to have seed sown, but now there is a callousness about your life. Ask the Lord to help you get back to the place where you can receive His Word as you should receive it.

## "BY THE WAYSIDE"

Where the Lord Jesus gave this parable, the people were very familiar with the terms He used. On the paths where people walked, there was hard soil. When they walked along those paths, they hardened the earth. Some seed fell on those hardened paths. It would lay there until the fowls of the air came and took it. It never took root.

The Lord said, "Some of you have hearts like that. You have hearts like a path, hardened, and trodden down. You have allowed your heart to get hard and calloused. You hear it, but you don't hear it."

When He interprets the parable, He says in verses eighteen and nineteen,

> *Hear ye therefore the parable of the sower. When any one heareth the word of the kingdom, and understandeth it not, then cometh the wicked one, and catcheth away that which was sown in his heart. This is he which received seed by the wayside.*

The wayside is this hardened path. This is the person who does not understand. Why does he not understand? Because the soil of his heart is hardened.

## "INTO STONY PLACES"

The second type of soil is shallow. The Word of God says in Matthew 13:20-21,

> *But he that received the seed into stony places, the same is he that heareth the word, and anon* [quickly, immediately] *with joy receiveth it; yet hath he not root in himself, but dureth for a while: for when tribulation or persecution ariseth because of the word, by and by he is offended.*

The stony place is not a place of rock, but a place where very little earth covers the rock. Here is a fellow who looks as if he has received it. He may have made a profession of faith, but his heart is like a stony place. He looks very joyous, but he learns there is more required of the Christian life than he first imagined. The Word of God speaks to him and challenges him but he says, "That is not for me."

Have you ever been to the place in your life when you heard the preacher talk about the way Christians should live and what Christians should do, and you said, "I'm not going to go that far with it"? Did you know that if you have the right kind of soil in your heart, then you will not say anything that will limit how far you will go with God? There should not be any reservation, any strings attached, or any lines drawn. If our hearts are right with God, we should say, "Whatever God shows me, I am going to do. I have already decided there is no limit to where I will let Him lead me."

## "AMONG THE THORNS"

The third heart is a heart that is crowded. Anything that crowds Christ out of your life is a thorn. Remember, it may even be something that is good. Others might say, "That is beautiful," but if it crowds Christ out, then it is a thorn. God's Word says in verse twenty-two, *"He also that received seed among the thorns is he that heareth the word; and the care of this world, and the deceitfulness of riches, choke the word, and he becometh unfruitful."*

You do not have to be a wicked person in the eyes of other people to be overly concerned about the riches of this world. Many people do not live for Christ as they should because they love money. What place does money have in your life? How much do you worry about it? How much do you talk about it? Do you believe that God is able to provide? Can you trust the Lord? Do you pay the tithe like a faithful Christian? Is money a problem because you have over-extended yourself financially? As we allow the Lord Jesus to speak to us, He will begin to convict us about how much emphasis we place on wrong things. A crowded heart is a heart where Christ has very little room. He is crowded out, and anything that crowds Him out is a thorn.

## *"INTO THE GOOD GROUND"*

We read also that some seed fell on good ground. The Bible says in verse twenty-three, *"But he that received seed into the good ground is he that heareth the word, and understandeth it; which also beareth fruit, and bringeth forth, some an hundredfold, some sixty, some thirty."*

Let us look at a parallel account of this in Mark chapter four. The Bible says in Matthew 13:23 that the good ground is a heart that understands. In Mark 4:20 the Bible says, *"And these are they which are sown on good ground; such as hear the word, and receive it."*

In the eighth chapter of Luke, we learn something else about this good ground. In each of these three Gospel records, God gives us one little key to this heart of good ground. It is a heart that understands. It is a heart that receives. In Luke 8:15 the Bible says, *"But that on the good ground are they, which in an honest and good heart, having heard the word, keep it, and bring forth fruit with patience."*

The *"good ground"* is a heart that understands, receives, and keeps. When you come to church and you listen to the preacher preach, do you understand? Whether or not you understand is an indication of what kind of heart you have. Do you have spiritual understanding? Have you cultivated your heart, or is your heart dull? I know that sometimes it is the speaker's fault, but there are times when the preacher pours out his heart, and the people do not get anything out of it. There are times when the preacher is in tune with God and he speaks the truth in love and in the power of the Holy Spirit, and the people do not get anything out of it. Examine your heart to see if you really have a spiritual understanding. This is an indication of what kind of soil you have in your heart. If you attend a Bible-preaching church, what you get out of it says much more about your heart than it does about your preacher.

Do you receive God's Word? Do you sometimes say, "There are things I need to make right with God. I have received the teaching. I have received the preaching." Are you that kind of person? This indicates what kind of soil you have in your heart.

Some people sit and listen all the time and say, "That's for someone else." Do you ever know that God is dealing directly with you? Do you ever think that the reason the message was preached was that God wanted you to hear it? This is an indication of what kind of heart you have.

The good soil keeps the Word of God. Most people leave church and forget what was said thirty minutes after they are gone. When God speaks to you by His Holy Spirit and you savor, you keep, you cradle what God has said, it is an indication of what kind of soil you have in your heart.

No wonder Christ said, "Let's get this parable of the sower straight." If I did not understand this parable of the sower, I would get very discouraged about the way people respond to God's Word. We need to keep the Word of God as it is sown in our hearts. Allow the Lord to use His Word to change your life.

# Chapter Three

# THE WHEAT AND THE TARES

he parable of the wheat and the tares is one of the greatest stories ever told. As Christ gives the explanation of this parable, a very tender scene unfolds. The multitude is dismissed and Christ enters into a house. His disciples go with Him and say, "Explain to us the parable of the tares. Tell us what this means." This is the second of the kingdom parables.

In Matthew 13:24-30 the Bible says,

> *Another parable put he forth unto them, saying, The kingdom of heaven is likened unto a man which sowed good seed in his field: but while men slept, his enemy came and sowed tares among the wheat, and went his way. But when the blade was sprung up, and brought forth fruit, then appeared the tares also. So the servants of the householder came and*

> *said unto him, Sir, didst not thou sow good seed in thy field? from whence then hath it tares? He said unto them, An enemy hath done this. The servants said unto him, Wilt thou then that we go and gather them up? But he said, Nay; lest while ye gather up the tares, ye root up also the wheat with them. Let both grow together until the harvest: and in the time of harvest I will say to the reapers, Gather ye together first the tares, and bind them in bundles to burn them: but gather the wheat into my barn.*

A little later, we come to verses thirty-six through forty-three of this same chapter where the Bible says,

> *Then Jesus sent the multitude away, and went into the house: and his disciples came unto him, saying, Declare unto us the parable of the tares of the field. He answered and said unto them, He that soweth the good seed is the Son of man; the field is the world; the good seed are the children of the kingdom; but the tares are the children of the wicked one; the enemy that sowed them is the devil; the harvest is the end of the world; and the reapers are the angels. As therefore the tares are gathered and burned in the fire; so shall it be in the end of this world. The Son of man shall send forth his angels, and they shall gather out of his kingdom all things that offend, and them which do iniquity; and shall cast them into a furnace of fire: there shall be wailing and gnashing of teeth. Then shall the righteous shine forth as the sun in the kingdom of their Father. Who hath ears to hear, let him hear.*

This is the parable of the wheat and the tares. Note an expression in the twenty-fifth verse, *"tares among the wheat."*

Christ explains this parable in verses thirty-seven through thirty-nine. First He tells us, *"He that soweth the good seed is the Son of man..."* Second, He says, *"The field is the world..."* Then He says, *"The good seed are the children of the kingdom..."* He tells us, *"The tares are the children of the wicked one..."* Fifth, He says, *"The enemy that sowed them is the devil..."* We learn that *"the harvest is the end of the world..."* And Christ also says, *"The reapers are the angels."*

We read about the Devil, the wheat and the tares, the good seed and the bad seed, and the idea that the servants are asking if they can pull the bad seed, the tares, out of the ground. The answer comes, "No, let them go to the harvest." What does all this mean? What understanding do we gain about the work of God from this particular parable?

As far as the story was concerned, they had no trouble understanding it. It was sort of a cruel joke. A man had sown his field with wheat. During the night, while he slept, an enemy came and sowed seed for tares.

Tares are weedy plants that grow in grain fields. They closely resemble wheat until the harvest time. Of course, a great lesson is gained. They look almost identical until the fruit comes. We are told that the root system of the tares is poisonous and entangles itself with the root system of the wheat. There is absolutely no way to pull the tares from the ground without destroying or disturbing the wheat.

> *They look almost identical until the fruit comes. We are told that the root system of the tares is poisonous and entangles itself with the root system of the wheat. There is absolutely no way to pull the tares from the ground without destroying or disturbing the wheat.*

What does it mean, that wheat is sown together with tares? Does it have anything to do with the idea that there are some people who say they are Christians but really are not? It certainly does, for some profess to be believers but are only imitators. In this parable we learn something of the apostasy among Christians, much like we are dealing with at this present time.

Let us lay down a few guidelines. We cannot take this parable and prove that we should allow heresy to continue within the local church. In this parable, Christ is not talking specifically about the church. He said, *"The field is the world."* Some people may say, "Well, in the church we have room for all kinds of things." No, we do not. We have room for one thing and that is doctrinal soundness. We find our doctrine in God's Word.

Do not attempt to use this parable to justify allowing people to teach various interpretations of Scripture in the same church. We must understand that there is one primary interpretation of any Scripture passage, given in its context. There may be many applications, but there is only one interpretation. As we agree on the particular interpretation, then let us teach it.

# THE WAR BETWEEN THE SEEDS

We learn from this parable of the war between the seeds. The Bible says that Christ spoke to His disciples and told them of the good seed and the bad seed. When they asked Him what it meant, He said, *"The good seed are the children of the kingdom; but the tares are the children of the wicked one."* There is a war between the seeds, the good seed and the bad seed. We are not only speaking of the Lord Jesus Christ and the Devil, but we are also talking about those who are children of God and those who are children of the Devil. All people are children of the Devil by nature and can only become children of God by faith in Jesus Christ. There is a battle going on between the seeds.

Let me remind you again that the Bible says in Genesis 3:15, *"And I will put enmity between thee and the woman, and between thy seed and her seed; it shall bruise thy head, and thou shalt bruise his heel."*

Each Christian has been born again of incorruptible seed, by the Word of God which liveth and abideth forever. All people who have not been born again of this incorruptible seed have another seed. They are children of the Devil by nature. All of us fall into that category by being part of the human race. We must be born from above, regenerated by the God of heaven and earth, to become part of His family.

*We cannot take this parable and prove that we should allow heresy to continue within the local church.*

In the eighth chapter of the Gospel according to John, the Lord Jesus spoke in verse forty-four about a certain kind of children. What He said was not to a group of degenerate-looking people, not to a group of adulterers, not to a group of murderers, not to a group of whoremongers, not to a group of drunkards, but He spoke these words to a very respectable-looking group of people. The Bible says in John 8:44,

> *Ye are of your father the devil, and the lusts of your father ye will do. He was a murderer from the beginning, and abode not in the truth, because there is no truth in him. When he speaketh a lie, he speaketh of his own: for he is a liar, and the father of it.*

Christ said, *"Ye are of your father the devil, and the lusts of your father ye will do."*

The word *parable* means "to place something alongside." Christ gives this story that is easily understood. He places alongside this story great spiritual truths that need to be understood.

He says, "The wheat seed has been sown. At night, the tares are sown. The farmer is excited about his harvest, anticipating that it will be a great one. Then he realizes that, coming up with the wheat, are tares. When he sees the fruit of the wheat, and he sees the fruit of the tares, he recognizes the difference between the wheat and the tares."

Christ explains to His disciples, "You are going to get excited as you go out and give the seed, preaching the Word of God. As you do, you are going to come face to face with this war between the seeds. The children of God and the children of the Devil are at war against one another."

# THE WORLD WILL NOT BE CONVERTED

It is our responsibility as believers to go *"into all the world, and preach the gospel to every creature"* (Mark 16:15). There is no doubt about this. However, we have already learned from the first of the parables in Matthew chapter thirteen that not everyone is going to be saved.

We also learn, from this parable, that there are many people among professing Christians who do not possess Christ. They look like the real thing; they start out like the real thing, but they prove, by the fruit of their lives, that they are not truly children of God.

Many people, even some Christians, believe that the world is going to get better and better. We hear phrases such as, "Let's win the world to Christ." There is no Bible basis for that expression. There are other expressions like, "Let's change the world for Christ." There is no biblical basis for this either. It is fantasy. We must approach this world with the idea that the entire world is not going to be saved, but we must reach as many people as possible with the gospel. Those that trust Christ as Savior will influence the world for Christ.

The Devil gets people to believe that they can win the world to Christ and change the world for Christ to bring in the kingdom. Many then become discouraged when it seems as if their efforts have failed. The truth is that Jesus Christ taught His disciples that as He Himself had been rejected, His message and His gospel would be rejected. Many would hear it, but few would believe it and receive it.

The world is not getting better and better. Evil men and seducers are waxing worse and worse. Even though we say we do not believe this idea of a better world, it affects our thinking to such a degree that we are tempted to be disobedient to God. We often want to extend the perimeters, widen the boundaries, take more people in, make it more pleasing and more interesting, and talk about an increasing number of Christians. We do this because we are still affected by this idea that we are finally going to win everyone to the Lord. It is not going to happen.

*There are many people among professing Christians who do not possess Christ. They look like the real thing; they start out like the real thing, but they prove, by the fruit of their lives, that they are not truly children of God.*

You may ask me, "Are you glad to say it is not going to happen?" No, but I know it is biblically accurate to say it will not happen. We still have the responsibility to evangelize the world. To evangelize the world is to give a clear presentation of the gospel to everyone.

Think about this parable. Think of being seated in the house with those disciples and listening to what Christ says to them. They are going out with the gospel into all the world, and they are going to preach the gospel to every creature.

How do you think they are going to feel when they are rejected? How do you think they are going to feel when other people begin to "mimic" what they are doing, when others begin to look like Christians but never get saved? How do you think they are going to feel when they go into a town of twenty thousand and twenty get saved? How do you think they are going to feel when they go into a place of five thousand and five get saved?

It is one thing to evangelize the world and give the gospel to everyone; it is another thing entirely to believe that everyone is going to be saved. The world is not going to be converted. The kingdom of our Christ is not coming from the earth up; it is coming from heaven down.

A false idea permeates our thinking, especially today, when it comes to the political realm. We think if we have a Christian President, Christian congressmen, Christian senators, Christian mayors, and Christian governors, we are going to have a Christian country. It is not going to happen. I believe we should vote in high moral standards and vote out low moral standards. For the most part, you can say high moral standards go with God-fearing, Bible-believing, Christian people. That is why we like to hear about Christian people taking their stand. However, let us stop thinking we can create a Christian world by electing Christian leaders.

From this parable, we learn that there are tares with the wheat. The world is not going to be converted. We do not need to labor under the mistaken idea that everyone is going to believe the gospel message.

We need an understanding of our biblical position. We must not compromise our biblical position for some idea of what we would like to see if that idea conflicts with what Jesus Christ taught His disciples.

We are biblicists. We believe that the real Christian position is a thoroughly biblical position. What we are declaring by this separatist position is that we are not going to compromise in order to broaden God's family and join with everyone in town who says he is a Christian, no matter what he believes.

Jesus Christ prepared His disciples by teaching them these parabolic teachings. One may say, "Doesn't it worry you that you can't work with everyone?" No, I have come to the place where if a man believes the Bible, and he separates himself unto the gospel, I can work with him. If he does not believe the Book and does not separate himself unto the gospel, I cannot work with him. You see, I have not become divisive. The other fellow is divisive because he refuses to believe the Bible. He says of me that I am divisive, intolerant, and bigoted because I will not work with him; but I want to be true to God and His Word. We are to love all people, but we are to love God more.

This parable is more than Christ saying to the disciples, "This is what the tares mean; this is what the wheat means. This is who the sower of the good seed is, and this is who the sower of the tares is." It gives us an understanding that the world is not going to be converted. Everyone is not going to be saved.

Do we want everyone to be saved? Of course we do, but not everyone is going to be saved. This is the clear teaching of the Word of God. I do not know if you have ever been exposed to liberalism, but I have. I have been in Bible classes in college where instructors taught that eventually everyone is going to get saved. They said things like, "Even though there is a hell, it is just a place where people go to get purified so they can go to heaven." Other statements were given such as, "We are all God's children, and finally everybody will get to God." This teaching is not biblical.

# THE WORK OF SATAN IS DECEPTION

Christ made a great point of saying to His disciples that the tares were with the wheat. They understood what these tares were like. They understood what they looked like. They understood that until the fruit came in the plant, one could not tell the difference. They had an understanding from this parable, that when they went out, there would be great imitators of the genuine. There would be counterfeiters of the reality, leaders who were not real. They knew that the Devil was going to do a work of deception.

How does the Devil do his deadliest work? It is not with drugs or drunkenness. He does his deadliest work with someone in a pulpit, who speaks articulately, is winsome, and says things that sound very good. They may even have a little truth mixed with their words to help with the deception, yet they speak a lie when it is judged by the standard of God's Word.

*The most dangerous deception is the deception that is closest to the truth.*

The work of Satan is deception. In Matthew 7:15 the Bible says, *"Beware of false prophets, which come to you in sheep's clothing, but inwardly they are ravening wolves."*

Christ said, *"Beware of false prophets."* How are they going to come? They are going to come looking like sheep, but they are not sheep at all; they are wolves. The work of Satan is deception. How do you know if a man speaks the truth? Ask, "Does his teaching agree with the witness of the Holy Spirit? Does it line up with the Word of God?"

In Matthew 24:4-5 Christ warns His disciples. He says, *"Take heed that no man deceive you. For many shall come in my name, saying, I am Christ; and shall deceive many."*

Verse eleven says, *"And many false prophets shall rise, and shall deceive many."*

Verse twenty-four says, *"For there shall arise false Christs, and false prophets, and shall show great signs and wonders; insomuch that, if it were possible, they shall deceive the very elect."*

The most dangerous deception is the deception that is closest to the truth. We are living in an awful age of apostasy, when many people profess Christianity but do not possess Christ. The tares are among the wheat.

In II Corinthians 11:13-15 the Bible says,

> *For such are false apostles, deceitful workers, transforming themselves into the apostles of Christ. And no marvel; for Satan himself is transformed into an angel of light. Therefore it is no great thing if his ministers also be transformed as the ministers of righteousness; whose end shall be according to their works.*

Remember, when Christ gave these parabolic teachings, Judas was numbered among the disciples. They were going to go out and meet others like Judas who were numbered among professing Christians, who say they know the Lord but do not really know the Lord. He was warning them that the Devil's work is the work of deception. Satan deceives.

The Bible warns us in II Peter 2:1, *"But there were false prophets also among the people, even as there shall be false teachers among you, who privily shall bring in damnable heresies, even denying the Lord that bought them, and bring upon themselves swift destruction."*

They are going to be among us too. The Bible says in Jude 3-4,

> *Beloved, when I gave all diligence to write unto you of the common salvation, it was needful for me to write unto you, and exhort you that ye should*

*earnestly contend for the faith which was once delivered unto the saints. For there are certain men crept in unawares, who were before of old ordained to this condemnation, ungodly men, turning the grace of our God into lasciviousness, and denying the only Lord God, and our Lord Jesus Christ.*

God said in the book of Jude that there are people who actually *"crept in unawares"* in the places where they lifted up Christ as the only Savior. These people crept in and finally said, "He is not the Savior."

Our Lord, as rejected King, spoke to His disciples, not only about this age of apostasy, but also about this period of time in this particular dispensation that will be characterized by awful apostasy as we move closer to the coming of Christ. He personally warned His own disciples even in that first century about what they would be facing.

When we were growing up, we may have thought our moms and dads were old-fashioned. Some of us may have thought our parents were too tough. Some of you may have wanted to attend a church where they did something besides preach and sing–at least something besides preaching the Bible and singing the old songs about the blood of Christ. Maybe you thought you would like to find a place where they did many other flashy things that were entertaining. These places had an atmosphere almost like the world, where they could applaud and laugh and behave like it was not a church. That kind of atmosphere, still calling itself Christian, is more apt to breed what we find in this parable.

In this age of apostasy in which we live, make sure you are saved. Be sure that you not only profess Christ, but also possess Christ. Realize that we are not trying to save the whole world; we are trying to get as many people in this world saved as possible before we go out of this world. Understand that the great work of Satan is the work of deception. Take your stand on the truth of the Word of God.

# The Wheat and the Tares

# A Grain of
# Mustard Seed

uring the days of Christ's ministry on earth, it was common to use the expression, *"a grain of mustard seed."* The mustard seed was the tiniest thing one could behold. Christ also spoke, at a different time, about faith as *"a grain of mustard seed."* In this passage, Christ speaks about *"a grain of mustard seed"* being placed in the earth and a plant growing.

A mustard seed placed in the earth produced a shrub, not a tree. It was an herb. As the Lord Jesus told this story, He talked of this seed producing a tree. No doubt the hearers thought, "That is unnatural." What does this mean? Let us look at this parable in Matthew 13:31-32,

> *Another parable put he forth unto them, saying, The kingdom of heaven is like to a grain of mustard seed, which a man took, and sowed in his field:*

*which indeed is the least of all seeds: but when it is grown, it is the greatest among herbs, and becometh a tree, so that the birds of the air come and lodge in the branches thereof.*

We had a great advantage in understanding the first two parables in Matthew chapter thirteen because Christ explained what each of the parables meant. We have no better explanation than the explanation the Lord Jesus gives. When we come to the third parable, He does not give an explanation; however, the story is easily understood. The hearers had no difficulty understanding that a man would take a grain of mustard seed, place it in the earth, and a shrub-like plant would grow. They had no difficulty understanding that it was the tiniest and the least of all seeds and that it would produce a certain type of plant or shrub. But when Christ said, "It became a tree," this was difficult for them to understand. He said that it became a tree so that the birds of the air could come and lodge in the branches.

We know that when Christ started His work with His disciples, it was a humble beginning. We do praise God for the growth of the church through the centuries. The Lord Jesus Christ came from heaven's glory and was born of a virgin. He lived a sinless life. He called disciples unto Himself. They gained His passion for the lost of the world and received His power to do the work He gave them to do. He commissioned them to go *"into all the world, and preach the gospel to every creature"* (Mark 16:15).

Through the centuries, multitudes of people have believed the gospel message and have been saved. We still have the responsibility to go into all the world and preach the gospel to every creature. It is our God-given assignment to do everything we can to take the message of Jesus Christ and His saving power to the billions of people who now live on the face of this earth.

There are two distinctly different ideas about the interpretation of this parable. The Lord Jesus spoke in the first two parables about the rejection of His message. Some people believe that He gave this third parable to encourage His disciples, telling them that they were going to be received until finally the whole world would be filled with the message of Christ. They say that the gospel is going to be received to the extent that Christianity will be like a great tree, and birds, supposedly good birds, will come and lodge in the tree and people will find refuge in the Lord.

This seems like a good idea, but there is another interpretation of this parable. The true interpretation is that this tree represents all those who march under the banner of Christendom. It is not all genuine Christianity, but what people might call Christian although it really does not line up with biblical Christianity. This tiny grain of mustard seed grows into a huge tree and birds come and lodge in it. In this great tree, under the banner of Christendom, evil and unbelief actually begin to lodge.

*We still have the responsibility to go into all the world and preach the gospel to every creature.*

I do not think that you have to guess which interpretation of this parable is true. Evil men and seducers are waxing worse and worse (II Timothy 3:13). We live in a world that is rejecting Christ. We are not going to be able to win the whole world to the Lord. Even though it is our responsibility to go into all the world and preach the gospel to every creature, more people are going to reject the gospel than people who receive the gospel. This is not a pleasant thought, but it lines up with the truth of the Bible.

Within the branches of what the world calls Christianity, all kinds of evils are lodging. In a book published in 1993 entitled *Christianity in Crisis* by Hank Hanegraaff, many public figures are named who are preachers, and their errors are identified. Some people found the statements in this book so hard to believe that they would not believe them. Because of this, the author made tapes of the preachers actually saying these things.

Kenneth Copeland is quoted as saying, "Satan conquered Jesus on the cross." Benny Hinn, a very popular preacher, is quoted as saying, "Never ever go to the Lord and say, 'If it be Thy will.' Don't allow such faith-destroying words to be spoken from your mouth." The Bible plainly teaches that we are to pray, "If it be Thy will." Frederick Price, who has a church or an assembly of about 16,000 members, is quoted as saying, "God has to be given permission to work in this earth on behalf of man. Yes, you are in control. So if man has control, who no longer has control?" He answers the question, "God no longer has control."

Kenneth Hagan, another popular preacher, is quoted as saying, "Man was created on terms of equality with God, and man could stand in God's presence without any consciousness of inferiority." Friends, all these statements are heresy. All these statements are biblically incorrect.

We see a beautiful program for children in a church like ours, and we think it is a great thing to teach them songs and have them sing in front of the church. It is a beautiful thing, but do you know the best thing we can do for these children? The best thing we can do is to make sure the church in which they grow up is a church that still proclaims the truth. Be sure they are going to a Sunday School class where they hear the Word of God and sing songs that are doctrinally correct. The greatest thing we can do for them is make sure that the truth God has given to us is the truth they are receiving.

We are living in a very deceitful period of time. I could give a long list of names of so-called preachers, none of whom line up with the Bible. They are teaching things that are fundamentally wrong–things that are untrue about salvation, who God is, what God does, and what we are to become; yet they are included in the broad picture of what is called Christianity.

This situation has become so serious that some people who call themselves fundamental, Bible-believing Christians really do not want to hear this. Some may say that these false teachers have good intentions. No, these people do not have good intentions. They seek to pervert the truth. They change the truth of God into a lie, and we need to sound the alarm.

Our Lord was preparing His disciples with these parables. This plant became a harboring place for all kinds of evil and non-Christian people who still call themselves Christian.

Please do not get the idea that you are the only person in the world who is right. However, be sure you are a part of the people in this world who still believe God's Word. We do not need to be intimidated by our critics into a cowardly attitude and refuse to speak the truth in love.

*Some may say that these false teachers have good intentions. No, these people do not have good intentions. They seek to pervert the truth. They change the truth of God into a lie, and we need to sound the alarm.*

In this deceitful world, there is much going on that is very close to the truth but is not true. Many who call themselves Christians do not believe that God the Father, God the Son, and God the Holy Spirit are co-equal, co-existent, and eternally existent, yet these people call themselves Christians and have tremendous followings.

As Christians, how are we to live and function in a world that is full of so much confusion? What do you think when you go into so-called Christian bookstores and find books that are anything but

Christian? What do you think when New Age material is sold in Christian bookstores? What do you think when people like Robert Schuller get on television and say that the real sin problem is low self-esteem. Friends, if you can do away with sin, you do not need a Savior. Many so-called Christian leaders are saying, "Just help people feel better about themselves." You may help them feel better about themselves for a while, but if they are not born again and washed in the precious blood of Jesus Christ, they are going to die and go to hell forever.

Who is the real enemy? It is the sweet, kind guy who gets up and says, "You are really not a sinner; you just have low self-esteem." Is he really a friend to people? What about the man who will speak the truth in love and tell people that God declares we are all guilty before Him and are going to die and go to hell if we do not trust Jesus Christ as our personal Savior? The man who tells the truth is the real friend. The truth must be spoken in love, but people need to hear the truth.

Let us imagine you have someone with you, and the two of you are taking a nature walk through the woods enjoying the day. Suddenly, you see coiled at the foot of your friend, a poisonous snake. You know that, if you call attention to it, you are going to alarm your friend. You may frighten him so badly that he will never want to go back into the woods; but if you are a friend, you are going to warn him.

## KNOW FOR SURE THAT YOU ARE A CHRISTIAN

Know that you have been born of the Spirit of God. Know for sure that you are saved. The Bible says in II Timothy 1:5-7,

> *When I call to remembrance the unfeigned faith that is in thee, which dwelt first in thy grandmother Lois, and thy mother Eunice; and I am persuaded that in thee also. Wherefore I put thee in remembrance that thou stir*

*up the gift of God, which is in thee by the putting on of my hands. For God hath not given us the spirit of fear; but of power, and of love, and of a sound mind.*

Everyone who calls himself a Christian is not a Christian. We need to know for sure that we have been born of the Spirit of God, that we have accepted Christ as our Savior. Paul said in verse eight, *"Be not thou therefore ashamed of the testimony of our Lord, nor of me his prisoner: but be thou partaker of the afflictions of the gospel according to the power of God."*

The term *"afflictions of the gospel"* is almost something we cannot even imagine, much less grasp. We have danced with the world so long that we suffer no *"afflictions of the gospel."* There is so much of the world in most churches that one cannot tell the difference between the church and the world. The music and the conduct in the church should be distinctively Christian. We need to know for sure that we are saved.

The Bible says in II Timothy 1:9-12,

> *Who hath saved us, and called us with an holy calling, not according to our works, but according to his own purpose and grace, which was given us in Christ Jesus before the world began, But is now made manifest by the appearing of our Saviour Jesus Christ, who hath abolished death, and hath brought life and immortality to light through the gospel: whereunto I am appointed a preacher, and an apostle, and a teacher of the Gentiles. For the which cause I also suffer these things: nevertheless I am not ashamed: for I know whom I have believed, and am persuaded that he is able to keep that which I have committed unto him against that day.*

Paul said, *"I know whom I have believed."* Do you know for sure that you have asked God to forgive your sin, and by faith have received the Lord Jesus Christ into your life? Do you know that you have been born into God's family?

The church is caught up in everything imaginable except getting the gospel to people. Sure, we should clothe the naked, feed the hungry, and care for the poor. But this should never be the goal. These things are always by-products of the goal. Getting the gospel to people is what we must be doing. When we make a by-product the goal, we weaken the goal. May God help us to remember what is most important. People need the Lord. Let us know for sure that we are saved.

# KNOW THE WORD OF GOD

This lies at the root of our problem today. Many people who profess to know the Lord Jesus know little or nothing of His Word.

In the fifth chapter of the book of Hebrews, there is something very important that demands our attention. How can we recognize error? How does a man discern between what is right and what is wrong, what is good and what is evil? Can one listen to someone preach and, when a wrong statement is made, know immediately that it does not line up with the Bible?

The reason millions of people swoon at the feet of false prophets is that these people do not know the Word of God. If they knew the Bible, they would be turned off immediately when they hear statements made that do not agree with God's Word.

The Bible says in Hebrews 5:11-14,

> *Of whom we have many things to say, and hard to be uttered, seeing ye are dull of hearing. For when for the time ye ought to be teachers, ye have need that one teach you again which be the first principles of*

*the oracles of God; and are become such as have need of milk, and not of strong meat. For every one that useth milk is unskilful in the word of righteousness: for he is a babe. But strong meat belongeth to them that are of full age, even those who by reason of use have their senses exercised to discern both good and evil.*

Look at the last verse again, *"But strong meat belongeth to them that are of full age, even those who by reason of use have their senses exercised to discern both good and evil."*

Note the word *"discern."* We have so little discernment today.

Recently, an article was written about the lady who was in the heart of a controversy concerning the decision of *Roe vs. Wade* that brought about legalized abortion in America. The woman claimed that she had been sexually assaulted by numbers of men back at the particular time the case came to the forefront. She admitted later that she had lied. She had been practicing immoral behavior and became with child without a husband. Not long ago, she supposedly made a

*Many people who profess to know the Lord Jesus know little or nothing of His Word.*

profession of faith and was baptized in someone's swimming pool, yet she practices a lifestyle that the Bible calls *"vile affection"* and *"abomination."* She is not in love with a man; she is in love with a woman. She said she would much rather give up her faith than give up her lover.

A great fuss has been made over such a prominent person supposedly changing opinions about abortion. Can a person like that who says, "I would rather give up my faith than give up my lover," really be a Christian? No! How can Bible-believing people get so excited about something like that? The answer is that those who got so excited about her "testimony" did not know God's Word.

> *The reason millions of people swoon at the feet of false prophets is that these people do not know the Word of God.*

In many seminaries and preacher-training institutions today, people are being taught how to speak in churches without using the Scriptures. We have gone from raw-boned, Bible preaching to a little drama on the Lord's day, followed by a "Christian" soap opera. People are being entertained because they have itching ears and that is what they want. We have a world in which the Devil and demons are running wild, and there is little discernment concerning the truth. Tracing the situation right back to the root of the problem, we find churches filled with people who know little or nothing of the Bible. One cannot be a discerning person without the Bible.

The world's ideas are secular; they are without God. Secular, worldly wisdom and agendas have crept into many churches. Worldly ideas about how to accomplish Christian work have come into our churches. Many attempt to organize and promote the church into existence. This is all void of the Spirit of God.

It challenges all of us in our wicked and deceptive world to know the Word of God. Knowing the Word of God gives us warning immediately when we hear something that does not agree with the Word of God. We do not have to study every evil in the world, but we must know the truth of the Word of God. The truth will reveal the evil.

## KNOW THE SPIRIT OF GOD

In I John 4:1-3 the Bible says,

> *Beloved, believe not every spirit, but try the spirits whether they are of God: because many false prophets are gone out into the world. Hereby know ye the Spirit of God: every spirit that confesseth that Jesus Christ is come in the flesh is of God: and every spirit that confesseth not that Jesus Christ is come in the flesh is not of God: and this is that spirit of antichrist...*

The prefix *anti-* can mean "against" or "instead of." The word *antichrist* is used to represent any teaching that is against or instead of Christ, or anyone who embodies a teaching that is against or instead of Christ. It is ultimately the person of the Antichrist. The Bible continues in verse three, *"...whereof ye have heard that it should come; and even now already is it in the world."*

One can get so terribly alarmed about so much evil in the world, so much confusion, so much deception, that he wonders if the wicked are actually winning. In case you get alarmed, the Bible says in verse four, *"Ye are of God, little children, and have overcome them: because greater is he that is in you, than he that is in the world."*

The wicked are not winning. They may be ahead in the fifth inning, but this game is going to the ninth. It may be the bottom of the ninth, but when the trumpet sounds, Jesus Christ is coming again. He has already conquered death, hell, and the grave. We are on His side and He is on ours; we have the victory.

We need to know the Spirit of God. There are many spirits, so how do you know the Spirit of God? The Spirit of God will not honor men above Christ. The Spirit of God honors Jesus Christ and confesses Him. The Spirit of God will magnify the Son of God. Remember I John 4:2 says, *"Every spirit that confesseth that Jesus Christ is come in the flesh is of God."*

This may seem like something that should not concern you, but it will concern you when someone you love gets caught up in

# LEAVEN HID IN MEAL

n Matthew 13:33 we find the fourth of the kingdom parables. Jesus Christ spoke this parable to His disciples along with the multitude. The Bible says, *"Another parable spoke he unto them; The kingdom of heaven is like unto leaven, which a woman took, and hid in three measures of meal, till the whole was leavened."*

You may think, "What could be so significant in one verse of Scripture?" There is great significance in this parable.

In this passage, our Lord speaks with His disciples and with all of us who read His Word about what is happening in our world under the banner of Christendom. He is not speaking here of the true church or of heaven but of all that profess to be Christian. Remember that everyone who professes to be a Christian is not a Christian.

There are two different ways that people interpret this parable. These two interpretations are opposite in meaning. The determining factor is in deciding whether the leaven is good or evil.

Those who believe the leaven is good teach from this parable that the whole world will ultimately be filled with good. They say that the world keeps getting better and better. As we examine this in the light of the Bible, we find that this is certainly not true. God's Word says in II Timothy 3:13, *"But evil men and seducers shall wax worse and worse, deceiving and being deceived."*

In this fourth parable of Matthew chapter thirteen, the Lord Jesus takes us on the inside and shows us the corrupting effect of infiltration. Realizing that there are two great differences in the way men look at this matter, you are going to be criticized for taking the Bible view. You might as well prepare for it. The Bible view is separation unto the Lord from the world.

This is the parable of the leaven hid in three measures of meal. The Bible says in Matthew 13:33, *"Another parable spake he unto them; The kingdom of heaven is like unto leaven, which a woman took, and hid in three measures of meal, till the whole was leavened."*

Leaven is spoken of seventeen times in the New Testament. Sixteen of those times, there is absolutely no question that the leaven represents evil or an evil influence. The seventeenth time is here in Matthew 13:33, and it is left to interpretation. The Bible says that leaven, or yeast, is added to the meal. Considering the other parables in the context of this verse of Scripture and knowing that all the other times the word is mentioned in the New Testament it represents evil, we are safe to say that the leaven represents evil in verse thirty-three of Matthew chapter thirteen.

Let us note the significance of the meal. The first time we find three measures of meal mentioned is in the Old Testament book of Genesis. In Genesis 18:1 the Bible says, *"And the LORD appeared unto him in the plains of Mamre: and he sat in the tent door in the heat of the day."* This passage tells us of Abraham being visited by these three guests, one of whom was the pre-incarnate Christ. As God speaks to Abraham, the Bible says in verses two through six,

> *And he lift up his eyes and looked, and, lo, three men stood by him: and when he saw them, he ran to meet them from the tent door, and bowed himself toward the ground, and said, My Lord, if now I have found favour in thy sight, pass not away, I pray thee, from thy servant: let a little water, I pray you, be fetched, and wash your feet, and rest yourselves under the tree: and I will fetch a morsel of bread, and comfort ye your hearts; after that ye shall pass on: for therefore are ye come to your servant. And they said, So do, as thou hast said. And Abraham hastened into the tent unto Sarah, and said, Make ready quickly three measures of fine meal, knead it, and make cakes upon the hearth.*

As the Lord was passing through, He announced to Abraham the birth of his son Isaac. Sarah laughed about the matter. Then, of course, in the nineteenth chapter of Genesis, we find the destruction of Sodom and Gomorrah. Abraham was deeply concerned about his nephew Lot. He questioned whether Lot was a true believer. However, the three measures of meal mentioned here have great significance because it is the first time to be mentioned in the Bible. The meal prepared for these heavenly guests represents our fellowship with God.

If we take this first mention of three measures of meal in the Bible and compare it to this parable in Matthew thirteen, we understand that our Lord has in mind our fellowship with Him being infiltrated by something evil.

The woman is also very significant in this parable. The Bible says, *"The kingdom of heaven is like unto leaven which a woman took and hid."* We should understand what this woman signifies. Her behavior is secretive and deceitful. This certainly does not sound like something that a godly person would do, to be deceitful or secretive. She hid the evil in the meal. The woman represents a false religious system. Her behavior is satanic, evil, and deceitful. In the book of Jude, verse four, the Bible says, *"For there are certain men crept in unawares, who were before of old ordained to this condemnation, ungodly men, turning the grace of our God into lasciviousness, and denying the only Lord God, and our Lord Jesus Christ."*

> *We must diligently guard our doctrinal soundness.*

The word *"crept"* denotes a secretive, deceitful action. The Lord Jesus told His disciples this parable about a woman who took three measures of meal, which typifies our fellowship with God, and the woman added an evil element in a deceitful manner.

Some Bible teachers believe that the seven parables in Matthew chapter thirteen correspond with the seven churches mentioned in chapters two and three of the Revelation of Jesus Christ. Parable number one corresponds with church number one, parable number two with church number two, and so forth. If there is some significance to this, let us look at church number four because we are studying parable number four. In Revelation 2:18 the Bible says, *"And unto the angel of the church in Thyatira write; These things saith the Son of God, who hath his eyes like unto a flame of fire, and his feet are like fine brass."*

This is the only time that the Lord refers to Himself as the Son of God in these letters to the seven churches. In these letters, the Lord refers to Himself by a different title. To the church in Thyatira He refers to Himself as the Son of God. The Lord Jesus declares in Revelation 2:19-23,

> *I know thy works, and charity, and service, and faith, and thy patience, and thy works; and the last to be more than the first. Notwithstanding I have a few things against thee, because thou sufferest that woman Jezebel, which calleth herself a prophetess, to teach and to seduce my servants to commit fornication, and to eat things sacrificed unto idols. And I gave her space to repent of her fornication; and she repented not. Behold, I will cast her into a bed, and them that commit adultery with her into great tribulation, except they repent of their deeds. And I will kill her children with death; and all the churches shall know that I am he which searcheth the reins and hearts: and I will give unto every one of you according to your works.*

The woman in this letter is named Jezebel. The historical Jezebel, the wicked queen of King Ahab, polluted the true worship of God's people by introducing false worship into their lives. God chose the name of this wicked person in history, Jezebel, to represent someone in the church or church age who pollutes what is true.

Why discuss all of this? Because everyone who says he is of the Lord is not of the Lord. Everyone who names the name Christian is not a Christian. We should be on guard spiritually because we are living in an age of apostasy. Everyone who professes Christianity and stands under the banner of Christendom is not a true believer.

From what we know of the Word of God, the Son of God, and the Spirit of God, we should test the things we hear to see if they are really of the Lord or not of the Lord. Even in our own independent Baptist movement, there are people who have a tendency to believe that a little leaven will not hurt. Some say, "So what if that person doesn't believe exactly what the Bible teaches, what does a little hurt?" A little hurts a great deal because it eventually pollutes everything. We must diligently guard our doctrinal soundness.

The Lord leaves no doubt about this leaven. He names it for us. We have learned that the leaven is evil, not good. It is introduced into the three measures of meal, which we believe represents our fellowship with God. This woman, by her deceitful behavior, hiding the leaven in the meal, shows us that it is not something good that is going on but something very evil.

## THE LEAVEN OF THE PHARISEES

When the Lord Jesus began to talk about this leaven, He warned us first of the leaven of the Pharisees. In Matthew 16:6 the Bible says, *"Then Jesus said unto them, Take heed and beware of the leaven of the Pharisees."*

I want people to know the truth. Do you know the truth? Do you know that you have been saved and heaven is your home? Do not be ashamed of the gospel, *"for it is the power of God unto salvation to every one that believeth"* (Romans 1:16). The only way we are going to heaven is to ask God to forgive our sin and by faith receive Jesus Christ as our personal Savior. It is the work of the Devil to distort this message by mixing something else with it. It is the work of the gospel, which is the power of God unto salvation, to save those who believe, calling out from the world a bride for the Lord Jesus Christ.

Jesus Christ said, *"Beware of the leaven of the Pharisees."* What is the *"leaven of the Pharisees"*? One of the great principles of learning the Bible is to compare Scripture with Scripture, so let us look at the Gospel according to Luke. In the first verse of the twelfth chapter, we will find what the Lord Jesus said specifically about the leaven of the Pharisees. The Bible says in Luke 12:1, *"In the mean time, when there were gathered together an innumerable multitude of people, insomuch that they trode one upon another, he began to say unto his disciples first of all, Beware ye of the leaven of the Pharisees, which is hypocrisy."*

The leaven of the Pharisees is hypocrisy. The hypocrite pretends to be something he is not. The Lord Jesus said, *"Beware."* We do not think that we are perfect, but we are trying to preserve and guard the truth and not mix it with error. We do not strengthen our position as Bible-believing, truth-loving people by uniting with everyone in the world who says he is a Christian. If we do this, we will weaken our position, not strengthen it. Tolerating a little leaven allows that leaven to leaven the whole lump. Infiltration eventually brings within our belief system things that at one time we thought we would never allow. You may say, "Well, so what if we have a missionary somewhere that doesn't believe the Bible. So he is not trying to get people saved; he is trying to do something else." When did you begin to think that way? We finally allow many things by believing that a little bit of evil does not hurt. A little leaven does hurt.

> *Tolerating a little leaven allows that leaven to leaven the whole lump.*

The Lord Jesus said, *"Beware of the leaven of the Pharisees, which is hypocrisy."* What about a hypocrite? He is not talking about an atheist. God's Word tells us in Psalm 14:1, *"The fool hath said in his heart, There is no God."* The atheist announces his cause. He says, "I don't even believe in God."

That man does not frighten those of us who are Christians by standing up and saying, "I don't believe any of this. I don't believe the Bible. I don't believe in God." We know where he stands. That man is not nearly as dangerous as the hypocrite.

A hypocrite is an actor. The word *hypocrite* comes from someone wearing a mask to pretend to be someone he is not. The real danger does not lie in the person who is outspoken about what he does not believe, or in his opposition to God and the truth of God's Word. The real danger lies in the person who pretends to be someone he is not while subtly working against what the Bible teaches. This is hypocrisy. God's Word says, *"Beware of the leaven of the Pharisees, which is hypocrisy."*

Hypocrites are some of the most winsome people in the world. Some of the most charming, charismatic people in the world are people who are tools of the Devil to leaven the meal. We need to be careful and discerning. We need to protect what God has given us.

*Some of the most charming, charismatic people in the world are people who are tools of the Devil to leaven the meal. We need to be careful and discerning.*

Do not be ashamed of being a Bible-believer. Do not be ashamed that some will accuse you of being narrow-minded because you believe the Bible and refuse to fellowship with those who say they are Christians but will not separate from those who promote error.

Know what you believe. You are not to make unnecessarily harsh statements and be rude, but know in your heart what you believe. Take a strong stand for your Lord. Love the Lord Jesus, love the lost people about you, and hate sin.

# THE LEAVEN OF THE SADDUCEES

In Matthew 16:6 the Bible says, *"Then Jesus said unto them, Take heed and beware of the leaven of the Pharisees and of the Sadducees."* The Sadducees were a leading religious group in the Lord Jesus' day. They did not believe in the resurrection or life after death. In Matthew 22:23 the Bible says, *"The same day came to him the Sadducees, which say that there is no resurrection, and asked him, Saying, Master, Moses said, If a man die, having no children, his brother shall marry his wife, and raise up seed unto his brother."*

The Sadducees were the religious liberals and promoters of false doctrine. In this incident, they told a story about a woman who had seven different husbands and questioned Christ concerning whose wife she would be in the resurrection. The truth is, they did not even believe in the resurrection. Who were they trying to fool? They introduced doctrinal error. They did not believe the truth.

People say today, "We don't want to hear doctrine." But we *must* hear doctrine! The Bible says in II Timothy 3:16, *"All scripture is given by inspiration of God, and is profitable for doctrine."*

This "leaven of the Sadducees" is so evident today in all these groups who are willing to lay aside "doctrinal differences" in order to fellowship. The Lord Jesus said, *"Beware."*

You may say, "I don't like to go to church where they teach doctrine." What are you talking about? You are talking about the leaven of the Sadducees. We are to believe what God teaches, not what we think. This is not only important, it is vital.

We need to be people who know the truth of God's Word, and we must judge what we hear by lining it up with the Word of God. One of the tremendous problems we face at this present time is that we are living in a biblically illiterate society, and the people who are all around us know little or nothing of God's Word. Many people have the idea that you can just believe anything as long as you have a great time. They believe in believing–it does not really matter what the belief happens to be. Going to many churches is like going to a religious pep rally just to be entertained or amused.

You may ask someone, "What did you get out of church?" He may reply, "Well, we had a great time." You may ask, "What did you learn?" He may say, "Well, it is not important what you learn." It *is* important. We must beware of the leaven of the Sadducees, which is doctrinal error. To de-emphasize doctrine is evidence of the leaven of the Sadducees.

# THE LEAVEN OF HEROD

In the Gospel of Mark, the Lord Jesus warns us about the leaven of Herod. In Mark 8:15 the Bible says, *"And he charged them, saying, Take heed, beware of the leaven of the Pharisees, and of the leaven of Herod."*

In Matthew twenty-two, there were three groups that tempted Christ: the Herodians, the Pharisees, and the Sadducees. When they all finished questioning Him, they finally said that from that day forward they would ask Him no more questions because no one could withstand Him. In that story, the Lord Jesus pronounced woes upon the religious system of His day. Christ said to beware of the leaven of the Pharisees, which is hypocrisy. He said to beware of the leaven of the Sadducees, which is doctrinal error. We should also guard against the doctrine of the Herodians, or the leaven of Herod. What is it? The leaven of Herod is worldliness. The Sadducees lived only for the present; the Pharisees were hypocrites, and the Herodians were worldly.

The world is not becoming more Christian; Christians are becoming more worldly. The ideas of the Herodians were purely political. They did anything to promote the famous Herodian family. Even though the family of Herod is dead, the idea that the world needs a political savior is very much alive today. The Lord Jesus Christ said in John 18:36, *"My kingdom is not of this world."*

I do not mind asking politicians, "What do you believe about the great moral issues of our day?" or saying, "Let's vote morality up and immorality down." If a man says he is for abortion, I am against what he supports. If a man says he is for homosexuality, then I am against what he supports.

However, the church of the living God has gone into great error today by becoming so politically involved. Many preachers have left the pulpit for politics. We want the best moral representatives we can get to represent us politically; but we must guard against putting our hope and trust in the things of this world and in any political system. We must not move our hope and trust from where it should be, which is in the Lord.

> *The church of the living God has gone into great error today by becoming so politically involved.*

God's work is not done through religious coalitions. If we are not careful, we get ideas like, "If we just had a great religious coalition, think what we could do." For example, there is something today called the "Christian Coalition." I do not belong to it. I am a Christian, but there are many people in that coalition who are not Christians. They would be much better off to call it a "conservative" coalition than to call it a "Christian" coalition. I have no problem calling it a conservative coalition, but I have a real problem calling it a Christian coalition because they fly the Christian flag over too many things that are not Christian. I appreciate the information that I receive about voting records and issues, but it is still not necessarily "Christian" in the definition of Scripture.

The only hope we have is not in an attempt to reinstate "moral values." The only hope we have is in a spiritual revival. When revival comes, the moral fiber will be raised on the tide of spiritual revival.

May God keep us from being infiltrated with the leaven of Herod, which is worldliness. The idea of allowing a little of the world into the church in order to reach the world does not come from the Lord;

it comes from the Devil. All of us are *in* the world, but as God's children we are not to be *of* the world. This world system is not a friend to biblical Christianity.

What does all this mean for people like us? It means that we need to stay with what God has given us to do, although we are going to be misunderstood at times. We must continue to try to lead people to Jesus Christ for salvation. We should be exemplary citizens in compassion, courage, and civility, but we must not be sidetracked by the power of politics.

Do you ever stop to think about the kind of world and the kind of pressure that our young people face? Do you ever think about the kind of things that bombard them? They face temptations that previous generations never faced. What can we do for them? We can make sure we stay with the Bible. We must not betray our youth by allowing the leaven of the Pharisees, the leaven of the Sadducees, or the leaven of Herod to creep in. We must not betray them with hypocrisy, false doctrine, or worldliness. The Lord Jesus said, *"Beware of these things."* May the Lord help us to heed His warning.

# THE HIDDEN TREASURE

s we come to the last three of these seven parables in Matthew chapter thirteen, the Lord is speaking only to His disciples. Notice in the beginning of this chapter, in Matthew 13:1, the Bible says, *"The same day went Jesus out of the house, and sat by the sea side."*

The Lord Jesus left the dwelling where He was abiding and went outside. He went *"out of the house."* Now notice the thirty-sixth verse of this same chapter. The Bible says, *"Then Jesus sent the multitude away, and went into the house: and his disciples came unto him, saying, Declare unto us the parable of the tares of the field."*

Christ explains the parable of the tares, but this passage tells us that He is now inside the house with His disciples. He encouraged them and explained to them the work of the Lord. In particular, He explained the work that God is doing between the First

Advent, or First Coming of the Lord Jesus, and His Second Coming, or Second Advent.

When we study God's Word, there are certain principles of study that we can apply to the Bible. If we are going to understand the Bible, the first thing we need to do is *read* it. We should read a portion of God's Word every day. We should also *search* the Scriptures. We should look for specific things in the Word of God. The third thing we should do is *compare Scripture with Scripture.* I love to read books. I have all kinds of commentaries, but the greatest commentary on the Bible is the Bible. The Bible explains itself. The way we understand the Scripture is by taking one passage and comparing it with another passage. For example, when we look in Matthew thirteen, we need to find out what some of these things mean. The way we are going to find out what they mean is to find them spoken of in other passages. As we look in those other passages, and compare them with this passage of Scripture, then we come to understand what these terms are all about.

> *The greatest commentary on the Bible is the Bible. The Bible explains itself.*

Next, we are to *memorize* Scripture. The psalmist said in Psalm 119:11, *"Thy word have I hid in mine heart, that I might not sin against thee."* We should systematically memorize Scripture. The younger a person is, the better he can memorize Scripture, but all of us should take the challenge to memorize portions of the Word of God.

The fifth thing we are to do is *meditate* on Scripture. This washes our mind. To recall Scripture and meditate on it renews our thinking.

We need to understand the importance of comparing Scripture with Scripture as we look at this passage. *"All scripture is given by inspiration of God, and is profitable"* (II Timothy 3:16). The first thing God's Word does is make us wise unto salvation. Then it teaches us doctrine. It reproves us. It corrects us. It instructs us in righteousness.

As we open the Bible, we must rightly divide the Word of Truth (I Timothy 2:15). The Word of God says in I Corinthians 10:32, *"Give none offence, neither to the Jews, nor to the Gentiles, nor to the church of God."*

Notice each of these three. God is either speaking to the Jew, to the Gentile, or to the church. When we read any of the 1,189 chapters of the Bible, we are going to be reading something that is given to the Jew, something that is given to the Gentile, or something that is given to the church. Keep this in mind. It may not all be "to me," but it is all "for me."

As Bible believers, we normally divide the entire human race into lost and saved people; but let us make a different division. As far as God is concerned, we are either dealing with the Jew, the Gentile, or the church. This will become clearer to us as we study the Scriptures. We will find the Jew, the Gentile, and the church.

> *God has always had a people to whom and through whom He works in this world.*

As we come to the forty-fifth verse of Matthew chapter 13, the Lord tells us more about the church. However, in the forty-fourth verse, we are dealing with Israel. For some people this holds no importance, but let us attempt to bring the importance of this matter into view.

God has always had a people to whom and through whom He works in this world. We live in a world with billions of people in this present hour, and the Lord wants to make Himself known. When God decided to make Himself known to humanity, He chose a man.

This man's name was Abraham. He lived in a place called Ur of the Chaldees. God led Abraham from Ur of the Chaldees to a place that He would show him. He did not tell Abraham where He was going to take Him; He simply said, "Follow me." By faith Abraham followed the Lord. God made a covenant with Abraham promising to do certain things. From Abraham God raised up the mighty nation of Israel, the people we know as the Jews.

> *We live in a world with billions of people in this present hour, and the Lord wants to make Himself known.*

In this present hour, there is no place on earth as vital to world affairs as the nation of Israel. In one sense, Israel is God's time clock. It is very important for us to understand that God has not forgotten the Jews. They are back in the land in blindness, but they are God's chosen people. To those people, God revealed Himself. He gave them the responsibility to make Him known to all other people in the world. They failed in that responsibility.

They failed so miserably that when Jesus Christ came to earth and was born among men, they rejected Him. The word *incarnate* means "robed in flesh." God's Word says in John 1:14, *"And the Word was made flesh, and dwelt among us."* Jesus Christ was born of the virgin Mary, who was a Jew; therefore, Jesus was also a Jew. He was the promised Jewish Messiah and Savior of the whole world. But *"He came unto His own..."* the Bible says, *"...and His own received Him not"* (John 1:11). He came into the world that He created, and the Jews, the people God actually chose to make Him known to the world, did not receive Him and did not know Him.

Their responsibility is to be used of God, to be God's representative to the world. God chose a place for them; the place He chose was the

Holy Land. That land is the crossroads of the world, a land bridge between three continents. God has a special purpose for Israel.

When Jesus Christ came to earth, He came to the Holy Land. God gave His Word to us through the Jews. Our Savior came through the Jewish line God promised. We enjoy so many things from God's Word and God's people that we never consider. We should always remember God's chosen people, the Jews.

Two thousand years have passed since Christ was born of a virgin, lived a sinless life, and died on the cross. He was buried and rose from the dead. He ascended to heaven and promised to come again.

The Jews, God's chosen people, were put aside. To use a Bible term, they were "hidden." God began to make no difference between Jew and Gentile, and we find the birth of the church that has continued to make Christ known through the centuries.

Our Lord took His disciples inside the house and gave them these few words in this parabolic teaching. He said in Matthew 13:44, *"Again, the kingdom of heaven is like unto treasure hid in a field; the which when a man hath found, he hideth, and for joy thereof goeth and selleth all that he hath, and buyeth that field."*

## THE TREASURE

If we are going to understand this parable, we are going to have to define some of these things. Let us notice the word *"treasure."* What is this treasure? God's Word says, *"The kingdom of heaven is like unto treasure hid in a field."*

We have no question about what the field is because verse thirty-eight says, *"The field is the world."* Knowing that the field is the world, we understand that there is a treasure hidden in the world.

For seven hundred years before Christ came to earth, the nation of Israel was not what God intended for it to be. When the Lord came into the world, Israel was a scattered people without a king; they were hidden. We believe this treasure to be God's people, Israel.

The Bible says in Exodus 19:3-5,

> *And Moses went up unto God, and the LORD called unto him out of the mountain, saying, Thus shalt thou say to the house of Jacob, and tell the children of Israel; ye have seen what I did unto the Egyptians, and how I bare you on eagles' wings, and brought you unto myself. Now therefore, if ye will obey my voice indeed, and keep my covenant, then ye shall be a peculiar treasure unto me above all people: for all the earth is mine.*

In Deuteronomy 7:6-8 He said,

> *For thou art an holy people unto the LORD thy God: the LORD thy God hath chosen thee to be a special people unto himself, above all people that are upon the face of the earth. The LORD did not set his love upon you, nor choose you, because ye were more in number than any people; for ye were the fewest of all people: but because the LORD loved you, and because he would keep the oath which he had sworn unto your fathers, hath the LORD brought you out with a mighty hand, and redeemed you out of the house of bondmen, from the hand of Pharaoh king of Egypt.*

God chose His people. This is the Lord's doing. In Psalm 135:4 the Bible says, *"For the LORD hath chosen Jacob unto himself, and Israel for his peculiar treasure."*

Israel is His *"peculiar treasure."* We need to give heed, as a nation, to how we treat the nation of Israel. These are God's chosen people. At present, they are in darkness. They are in blindness, and we are going to find that they are in hiding. This treasure is the nation of Israel, God's chosen people.

# THE TREASURE HIDDEN

In Matthew 13:44 the Bible says, *"Again, the kingdom of heaven is like unto treasure hid in a field."*

This treasure is hidden. Its existence is insignificant to the world because it is hidden; it is unnoticed. Remember that this treasure is Israel, God's chosen people. Think about this treasure, *"...hid in a field; the which when a man hath found, he hideth."*

What about the Messiah? What about Christ coming and delivering us? Is that what He came to do two thousand years ago? The Bible says, *"He came unto his own, and his own received him not"* (John 1:11). The wheels of God's program for Israel did not grind to a screeching halt with the rejected Messiah. Instead, Israel was simply set aside for a time.

To get an idea about Israel being scattered and hidden, let us look at I Peter 1:1-2. The Bible says,

> *Peter, an apostle of Jesus Christ, to the strangers scattered throughout Pontus, Galatia, Cappadocia, Asia, and Bithynia, elect according to the foreknowledge of God the Father, through sanctification of the Spirit, unto obedience and sprinkling of the blood of Jesus Christ: Grace unto you, and peace, be multiplied.*

We call the last nine books of the New Testament the Hebrew Christian church epistles. The primary audience of these books was converted Jews. As they were addressed in I Peter 1:1 we read, *"Peter, an apostle of Jesus Christ, to the strangers scattered throughout Pontus, Galatia, Cappadocia, Asia, and Bithynia."* The

Jews were scattered throughout the earth. They were "hidden." We call this the Diaspora, or the dispersion of the Jews.

# THE MAN WHO FOUND THE TREASURE

The Jews were hidden, scattered, and dispersed. They are the treasure hidden in the world. Notice the man mentioned in the parable. Let us look in verse forty-four of Matthew thirteen, *"...the which when a man hath found..."*

Who is this man? This man is none other than Jesus Christ! If you interpret this man to be anyone other than Jesus Christ, nothing really makes sense in the parable. The Lord Jesus came unto His own. When He came to His own they were scattered, hidden in a field. The field is the world. Notice something interesting. When He came unto His own and found them scattered throughout the world, hidden in a field, He found them and He hid them.

# THE TREASURE HIDDEN AGAIN

To be hidden is not to be gone or lost forever. The Bible says, *"...when a man hath found, he hideth..."*

I can only imagine how Christ felt when He came and offered Himself to His own and was rejected. Matthew 21:43 is a verse which helps us to understand this subject. The Bible says, *"Therefore say I unto you, The kingdom of God shall be taken from you, and given to a nation bringing forth the fruits thereof."*

There was a time when the Lord Jesus Christ announced to the Jews that they had failed in God's work of making the Lord known. He told them that was why they were redeemed, why God chose them, why God called Abraham from Ur of the Chaldees, why God gave Abraham the son Isaac, and why God gave Isaac Jacob, and why Jacob had sons, and why they went down into Egypt. God raised the mighty nation of Israel out of Egypt, and to them and through them the Lord wanted to make Himself known to all the world.

This is why God placed them in the geographical place where He wanted them. This is why God revealed Himself to them. This is why God has made Himself known. To them God gave the Savior so that to them and through them all the world would hear about Jesus Christ and have the opportunity to be saved, but they failed.

In Matthew 13:45, we see the church. God did not stop His work with a rejected Israel; His work continues through His own when Jew and Gentile are all made one through the blood of Christ and His church. In Matthew 13:44 the Bible says, *"Which when a man hath found he hideth it."*

Israel is hidden again, set aside. The real commentary on this verse is found in the ninth, tenth, and eleventh chapters of Romans. If you read through the ninth chapter of the book of Romans, you find that God actually has chosen the nation of Israel. God selected them as His chosen people. In Romans 9:14 the question is asked, *"What shall we say then? Is there unrighteousness with God? God forbid."*

> *The wheels of God's program for Israel did not grind to a screeching halt with the rejected Messiah. Instead, Israel was simply set aside for a time.*

Is this something unrighteous that God has done, that He has chosen a people above all people? No, God can only do right. It is right that God chose them.

When we come to the tenth chapter, we find that God has set the Jews aside. During this church age, how does God deal with the Jews? We find in the twelfth verse of Romans chapter ten, *"For there is no difference between the Jew and the Greek: for the same Lord over all is rich unto all that call upon him."*

People are saved today, Jew and Gentile, by believing on the Lord Jesus Christ and trusting Him as Savior. But is God finished with Israel? No.

We come to Romans chapter eleven and the Bible says in verses five and six,

> *Even so then at this present time also there is a remnant according to the election of grace. And if by grace, then is it no more of works: otherwise grace is no more grace. But if it be of works, then is it no more grace: otherwise work is no more work.*

What about these Jews? In verse twenty-five the Bible says, *"For I would not, brethren, that ye should be ignorant of this mystery..."*

The Jews are hidden. The Lord Jesus came unto them. He found them in the world. They rejected Him. When He found them, He hid them. They are still set aside.

Do you know there is coming a day, according to the Revelation of Jesus Christ, when 144,000 Jews will be flaming evangelists preaching the gospel during the Tribulation period? God is not finished with them. He does not want us to be ignorant of this mystery. The Bible says, *"...lest ye should be wise in your own conceits, that blindness in part is happened to Israel, until the fulness of the Gentiles be come in."*

When the Bible speaks of *"the fulness of the Gentiles,"* God is dealing with this period of time when the Holy Spirit is calling out a bride. We are looking for our heavenly Bridegroom, the Lord Jesus. This fullness of the Gentiles speaks of this time when God is calling out a bride and every person who is a part of the bride is saved and the bride is complete. When the last one is saved, God will catch His bride away.

We read the term *"the times of the Gentiles"* in Luke 21:24. This term refers to the time period in which God has allowed Gentile nations to rule the world. It began with the Babylonians. Following the Babylonians, the Medes and Persians ruled, then the Greeks, and then the Romans.

In the book of Daniel, chapter two, King Nebuchadnezzar had a dream. In his dream he saw an image made of different metals, diminishing in value as they went from head to toe. After Nebuchadnezzar had the dream, he forgot it. He wanted his wise men, soothsayers, and astrologers to tell him about his dream. They could not tell him, so he said, "I will kill them all."

Daniel sought the Lord, prayed, and interpreted the dream. In his interpretation of the dream, God unfolds for us this period of time known as the "times of the Gentiles." This will help you understand your Bible.

In Daniel 2:10-13 the Bible says,

> *The Chaldeans answered before the king, and said, There is not a man upon the earth that can show the king's matter: therefore there is no king, lord, nor ruler, that asked such things at any magician, or astrologer, or Chaldean. And it is a rare thing that the king requireth, and there is none other that can show it before the king, except the gods, whose dwelling is not with flesh. For this cause the king was angry and very furious, and commanded to destroy all the wise men of Babylon. And the decree went forth that the wise men should be slain; and they sought Daniel and his fellows to be slain.*

In verses sixteen through nineteen the Bible says,

*Then Daniel went in, and desired of the king that he would give him time, and that he would show the king the interpretation. Then Daniel went to his house, and made the thing known to Hananiah, Mishael, and Azariah, his companions: that they would desire mercies of the God of heaven concerning this secret; that Daniel and his fellows should not perish with the rest of the wise men of Babylon. Then was the secret revealed unto Daniel in a night vision. Then Daniel blessed the God of heaven.*

The Bible says in verses twenty-seven through twenty-nine,

*Daniel answered in the presence of the king, and said, The secret which the king hath demanded cannot the wise men, the astrologers, the magicians, the soothsayers, show unto the king; but there is a God in heaven that revealeth secrets, and maketh known to the king Nebuchadnezzar what shall be in the latter days. Thy dream, and the vision of thy head upon thy bed, are these; as for thee, O king, thy thoughts came into thy mind upon thy bed, what should come to pass hereafter: and he that revealeth secrets maketh known to thee what shall come to pass.*

God clearly explains that this dream is going to reveal things to come, things that are hereafter. As Daniel interprets the dream, there is a head of gold. In that head of gold, we have pictured for us the world empire of Babylon led by Nebuchadnezzar. As we read further, we find the Medo-Persian empire pictured in the chest and arms of silver. Then the Greeks and their world empire are pictured in the mid-section of brass. The legs of iron picture for us the Roman empire. We move from gold, to silver, to brass, to iron, down to the toes of clay and iron mixed.

There is coming another world empire. This is what everyone is talking about today. World leaders are meeting and saying that we are willing to break down national boundaries, pledging allegiance in some parts of our own nation, not to the flag of the United States, but to the flag of the United Nations.

The world is looking for one great world empire again. It is on many world leaders' lips and in their thinking. Do you know who the leader is going to be? He will be the Antichrist. We are standing at the door of the fulfillment of this prophecy.

> *Let us look for and love the appearing of Jesus Christ.*

Let us look for and love the appearing of Jesus Christ. When the last person gets saved, the bride of Christ will be complete and the trumpet will sound. The Lord will come, and we will be caught out to be with Him. This will be the fullness of the Gentiles. The Bible says that this blindness in Israel is going to happen until the fullness of the Gentiles. In other words, there will be a time when their eyes will be opened. Just as Joseph was recognized by his brethren, Jesus Christ is going to be recognized by His brethren, the Jews. Their blindness will be gone. We are living near the time of the fullness of the Gentiles.

## THE MAN FOR JOY SOLD ALL THAT HE HAD

When we look at this parable, the Bible says that for joy, this same man whom we recognize to be Jesus Christ, *"goeth and selleth all that he hath, and buyeth that field."* This can be simply explained–He loves us. The Bible says in John 3:16, *"For God so* loved the world, that he gave his only begotten Son, that whosoever believeth in him should not perish, but have everlasting life."

God loves you. He loves His people Israel. Jesus Christ is talking about Himself in this parable. *"For joy thereof goeth and selleth all that he hath."* Why? To buy the field. The field? Yes, the treasure is in the field. If you get the field, you not only get the treasure, but you get everything in the field. The Jews are in the field, but the field is the world. He bought the whole world. What does this mean? The Bible says in Hebrews 12:2, *"Looking unto Jesus the author and finisher of our faith; who for the joy that was set before him endured the cross, despising the shame, and is set down at the right hand of the throne of God."*

>
>
> *Christ is our mercy seat. He is our place of salvation and mercy. He is the One who satisfied the holiness of a just God who demanded payment for sin.*

This verse says, *"...for the joy that was set before him..."* What joy? The humiliation of incarnation, when God became a man. What joy? Being misunderstood, mocked, and ridiculed all of His life on this earth. He was called a child born of fornication (John 8:41). What joy? To be rejected and spat upon, crowned with thorns, beaten, and bruised. What joy? For God to be robed in flesh, to stand before vile, wicked, religious priests and be condemned to die. What joy was there when Jesus Christ delivered Himself into the hands of sinners and allowed Himself to be nailed to a cross? He bore the sin of the whole world and actually became sin for us. The billows of God's wrath punished every awful, vile, ungodly, wretched, hellish sin that any man ever committed. Jesus Christ bore our sin debt in His own body on the cross. God's wrath rolled on His own Son on the cross. What joy is there in that?

The Bible says in the parable in Matthew 13:44, *"For joy thereof goeth and selleth all that he hath, and buyeth that field."*

The Bible says in Hebrews 12:2, *"For the joy that was set before him endured the cross, despising the shame."*

This means He counted it as nothing, less than nothing. What joy is there in that? The joy came because that field, which is the world, and what is in that field, which is the treasure, was so precious to Him. He sold all He had. What does that mean? It means He had nothing more to give. He could not give any more than He gave. He gave Himself. He gave everything. We could not get anything else from Him; He gave His life. There was nothing else to drain from Him; He shed His life's blood. He did it for joy, the joy of redeeming us.

We get happy sometimes when we see someone whom we have prayed for get right with God. It may be some mother's son. Some mom and dad may have joined hands beside a bed, weeping and crying out, "God, please save our boy, save our girl." A wife may pray, "Save my husband. Bring him back." A husband may pray for his wife. Sometimes children pray for their moms and dads the same way. We get hilariously happy and joyous when we see God do something for someone like that whom we are so burdened for and we love so very much. Every time we see God save someone like that and change someone's life, we get a little taste in our hearts of the joy that Jesus Christ talks about.

## THE MAN BOUGHT THE FIELD

Finally notice that He bought the whole field. The Bible says in I John 2:1-2, *"My little children, these things write I unto you, that ye sin not. And if any man sin, we have an advocate with the Father, Jesus Christ the righteous: and he is the propitiation for our sins..."*

Christ is our mercy seat. He is our place of salvation and mercy. He is the One who satisfied the holiness of a just God who demanded payment for sin. God's Word says, *"...and not for ours only, but also for the sins of the whole world."*

In the language of the parable, it would say, "for the sins of the whole field." Salvation is for everyone. Do you know what the Lord Jesus was saying to those disciples? He was saying, "I am going to the cross." By the way, He could not purchase the field until He sold all that He had. He wanted the treasure. He wanted the field. He wanted them to believe on Him. He wanted to save everyone of them. He wanted everyone in the world to know Him because God is *"not willing that any should perish, but that all should come to repentance"* (II Peter 3:9). But He could not get the field or the treasure in the field until He sold all that He had.

It was necessary for Christ to go to Calvary and give His all to provide salvation for the world. Those disciples inside that house were being told, "Go anywhere you want in the field, into all the world, and tell anyone you meet about the Son of man who came from heaven and shed His blood, died for his sin, and purchased his salvation. It is paid in full. All he has to do is receive it." What a precious parable–the hidden treasure.

God touched my heart to think about this man, our Savior, selling all He had to buy the field. If He had not, there would be no salvation. I want to thank the Lord that He gave His blood. I want to be more of what I should be for Him. Do you? I thank God that I can be more of what I should be because of what He has done for me. He enables me because of what He has done for me.

> *Again, the kingdom of heaven is like unto treasure* [Israel] *hid* [scattered everywhere] *in a field* [the world]*; which when a man* [the Lord Jesus] *hath found* [He came to the earth.], *he hideth* [He hid it because they rejected Him. He set them aside for a time.], *and for joy thereof goeth and selleth all that he hath* [He

gave absolutely everything. Christ went to Calvary and bled and died. Why?], *and buyeth that field.*

He did it so He could purchase us with His own blood. Hallelujah, what a Savior!

# One Pearl of Great Price

 n the first four of these kingdom parables in Matthew thirteen, our Lord concentrates on the work that the Devil is doing in the world between Christ's First Coming and His Second Coming, or His First and Second Advents. When we come to the fifth of these parables, the Lord takes His disciples into the house and speaks privately with them. As He does, He tells them, not what Satan is doing, but rather what He is doing in the world between His First Coming and His Second Coming.

Next we come to the sixth of these parables. The Bible says in Matthew 13:45-46, *"Again, the kingdom of heaven is like unto a merchant man, seeking goodly pearls: who, when he had found one pearl of great price, went and sold all that he had, and bought it."*

Notice the expression in verse forty-six, *"one pearl of great price."* We need to consider the fifth and sixth parables together.

Let us review the fifth parable. In Matthew 13:44 the Bible says, *"Again, the kingdom of heaven is like unto treasure hid in a field; the which when a man hath found, he hideth, and for joy thereof goeth and selleth all that he hath, and buyeth that field."*

When Jesus Christ took His disciples into the house and told them this fifth parable, He told them about His work. The treasure He speaks of is Israel, the Jew. God divides all the world into the Jew, the Gentile, and the church (I Corinthians 10:32).

*This One, Jesus of Nazareth, is the promised Messiah, presented Himself as King of the Jews; but the representatives of Judaism rejected their King.*

The Bible says the treasure was hidden in a field. We know that when Christ came the Jews were scattered throughout the world. *"He came unto his own, and his own received him not"* (John 1:11). The Bible says in the forty-fourth verse, *"The kingdom of heaven is like unto treasure hid in a field; the which when a man hath found, he hideth."*

It was hidden. He found it, and then He hid it. This speaks of when Christ came unto His own, and His own received Him not. He was the promised Messiah, the fulfillment of everything God had promised about the coming of a Savior. Can you imagine how these followers of Christ felt when the religious leaders of their day rejected the Messiah? They must have thought, "Does this mean the end of God's program? Does it mean that Christ failed?"

The Bible says He found the treasure hidden, and when He found it, He hid it. God is not finished with the Jews. They are hidden. The significance they once held in the world, being the people to whom and through whom God made Himself known to all the world, for this time has been set aside. However, they are set aside only for a while.

The Bible says that this One who came to them is the One who found them and hid them in the field. We know that Christ tells us in verse thirty-eight that the field is the world, so they are hidden in the world. This same One that found them, hid them, *"and for joy thereof goeth and selleth all that he hath, and buyeth that field."*

This is a picture of Calvary. The Lord Jesus Christ gave all that He had. He shed His life's blood not just for the sins of a few but for the sins of the whole world. He tasted death for every man.

We understand what the fifth parable means, and when we come to the sixth parable, we are dealing with a pearl, not with a treasure. It is not just a pearl, but the Bible calls it, *"One pearl of great price."*

There are many who have the idea that this pearl of great price is the Person of the Lord Jesus Christ. When we finish this study, you will realize that the pearl is not Christ, but rather what Christ gave Himself to purchase.

The Bible says, *"Again, the kingdom of heaven is like unto a merchant man, seeking goodly pearls..."* We need to understand who that merchant man is if we are going to understand the parable. The Bible says, *"...who, when he had found one pearl of great price..."* We need to know what that one great pearl is.

Then the Bible says that He *"went and sold all that he had, and bought it."* I think by now this expression is easy for most of us to understand as it relates to the work of Christ and what He came to do. Keep in mind that the Lord Jesus had Jewish followers. Even when Andrew brought his brother Simon to Christ, he brought him with this good news, *"We have found the Messias, which is, being interpreted, the Christ"* (John 1:41). Finally all the prophecies had been fulfilled in the coming of the Savior.

Christ was born of a virgin. He was born in Bethlehem. He was of the tribe of Judah, of the family of David. This One, Jesus of

Nazareth, the promised Messiah, presented Himself as King of the Jews; but the representatives of Judaism rejected their King.

I recall the conversation on the Emmaus road in Luke 24 after the death, burial, and resurrection of Jesus Christ. Those two Emmaus road disciples said in Luke 24:21, *"We trusted* [past tense] *that it had been he which should have redeemed Israel."* Did God's program fold up and finish when the Jews rejected Christ as Messiah at His First Coming? As we stand 2,000 years later and look back across history, we understand that God has a marvelous program going on now, even while the Jews are set aside.

If we are going to understand this parable, we need to look at John chapter ten. Our Lord spoke of the Good Shepherd. The Bible says in verses six through sixteen,

> *This parable spake Jesus unto them: but they understood not what things they were which he spake unto them. Then said Jesus unto them again, Verily, verily, I say unto you, I am the door of the sheep. All that ever came before me are thieves and robbers: but the sheep did not hear them. I am the door: by me if any man enter in, he shall be saved, and shall go in and out, and find pasture. The thief cometh not, but for to steal, and to kill, and to destroy: I am come that they might have life, and that they might have it more abundantly. I am the good shepherd: the good shepherd giveth his life for the sheep. But he that is an hireling, and not the shepherd, whose own the sheep are not, seeth the wolf coming, and leaveth the sheep, and fleeth: and the wolf catcheth them, and scattereth the sheep. The hireling fleeth, because he is an hireling, and careth not for the sheep. I am the good shepherd, and know my sheep, and am known of mine. As the Father knoweth me, even so know I the*

> *Father: and I lay down my life for the sheep. And other sheep I have, which are not of this fold: them also I must bring, and they shall hear my voice; and there shall be one fold, and one shepherd.*

When the Lord Jesus said, *"Other sheep I have, which are not of this fold,"* He meant other than the nation of Israel. He came and presented Himself to His own, and His own received Him not; but He said, "I have other sheep which are not of this fold. I have other sheep, those who are redeemed by the precious blood of the Lamb, who are not of this fold." Who are those other sheep? They are the Gentiles who believe on the Lord Jesus Christ to be saved.

In Matthew, chapter sixteen, our Lord introduces a new term to His disciples. The Bible says in Matthew 16:13-14,

> *When Jesus came into the coasts of Caesarea Philippi, he asked his disciples, saying, Whom do men say that I the Son of man am? And they said, Some say that thou art John the Baptist: some, Elias; and others, Jeremias, or one of the prophets.*

When they said He was John the Baptist, no doubt they thought about how He preached and spoke with authority. They must have thought, "No one speaks like that except John the Baptist. He must be John the Baptist." They said, "But some say You are Elijah." When they saw the miracles that the Lord Jesus performed they said, "He must be Elijah. No one is such a miracle-working prophet except Elijah." They said, "Others say you are Jeremiah." Jeremiah was known as the weeping prophet. When they saw the tears and compassion of Christ, they said, "He must be Jeremiah." The Bible continues in verses fifteen through eighteen,

> *He saith unto them, But whom say ye that I am? And Simon Peter answered and said, Thou art the Christ, the Son of the living God. And Jesus answered and said*

*unto him, Blessed art thou, Simon Bar-jona: for flesh and blood hath not revealed it unto thee, but my Father which is in heaven. And I say also unto thee, That thou art Peter, and upon this rock I will build my church; and the gates of hell shall not prevail against it.*

We need to keep these words, *"my"* and *"church,"* together. Christ said, *"I will build my church."* I think it is always helpful to remark that He did not say, "I will build *your* church," or "*You* will build My church." There is so much discussion today about church growth and producing church growth. The Bible says that God gives the increase. If men try to take credit for it, they are robbing God of the glory that belongs to Him. The apostle Paul said in Galatians 6:14, *"But God forbid that I should glory, save in the cross of our Lord Jesus Christ."* At best we are nothing.

> *Christ said, "I will build my church."*

The Lord Jesus said, *"I will build my church."* When the disciples heard that, it had special significance. Christ was introducing something to these Jewish minds that He would continue to unfold. It was the same thing He introduced to them in this sixth kingdom parable when He spoke of the *"one pearl of great price."*

When Christ finished the parables, the disciples said that they understood everything He taught them; the truth is they really did not understand everything He taught them. Even after He died, was buried, and rose from the dead, they still did not understand. He had to say to them, *"It behoved Christ to suffer."* He did not come just to rule and reign. He is going to rule and reign, but He came first to bleed and die. There is suffering before the crown.

When we go back to this parable in Matthew 13, let us consider what our Lord is teaching His disciples inside that house to encourage them. He taught them in the first four parables that the

Devil is going to run rampant. What does He teach His disciples after that? They knew they were going to have opposition from the Devil, but they needed to know that the church will never be overcome by the Devil. It will never be conquered by Satan.

God has a treasure; that treasure is Israel; but thank God He also has *"one pearl of great price,"* which is His church. I am part of that *"pearl of great price."* People minimize the church today. The body of Christ is minimized; but you cannot minimize it and grasp the full significance of this parable of *"one pearl of great price."*

The Bible says, *"Again, the kingdom of heaven is like unto a merchant man* [Jesus Christ is that merchant man.] *seeking goodly pearls: who, when he had found one pearl of great price, went and sold all that he had, and bought it."*

In I Corinthians 10:31-32 the Bible says, *"Whether therefore ye eat, or drink, or whatsoever ye do, do all to the glory of God. Give none offence, neither to the Jews..."*

From the bosom of Abraham, God raised up the mighty nation of Israel. We see the significance of God calling a man from the Ur of Chaldees by the name of *Abram.* God led Abram. God promised him a son, and in his old age He gave him a son, Isaac. To Isaac He gave Jacob, and to Jacob He gave sons. Jacob's name was changed to *Israel,* and Jacob and his sons went down into Egypt. They came out of bondage in Egypt after four hundred years. They came out as a mighty nation called Israel. God made a covenant promise to Abraham that He would do certain things, and through these people He would make Himself known to the whole world. These are God's people, the Jews. They are still God's chosen people. The Lord is not finished with them.

The Bible says, *"...nor to the Gentiles..."* God kept a leash on Gentile nations so that no Gentile nation could rule the world until Babylon ruled the world. Once Babylon began ruling the world, the *"times of the Gentiles"* began. The world empire of Babylon was conquered by the Medes and Persians. The Medes and Persians were followed by the Greeks. Alexander the Great and the Greeks were followed by the Romans. The Romans were the last great world empire. Others, like Napoleon and Hitler, have tried to have another world empire, but no one has fully succeeded. However, another world ruler is coming. He will be the Antichrist. Before he comes, we believe the *"fulness of the Gentiles"* will come in. The last person will get saved to make up the bride of Christ. That leads us to see, *"...nor to the church of God."*

God deals with either the Jews, the Gentiles, or the church. When we deal with the church, there is neither Jew nor Gentile, but *"one pearl of great price."* In I Corinthians 12:12-14 the Bible says,

> *For as the body is one, and hath many members, and all the members of that one body, being many, are one body: so also is Christ. For by one Spirit are we all baptized into one body, whether we be Jews or Gentiles, whether we be bond or free; and have been all made to drink into one Spirit. For the body is not one member, but many.*

The body is one, just as there is one pearl of great price. In Ephesians 2:14-15 the Bible says,

> *For he is our peace, who hath made both one, and hath broken down the middle wall of partition between us; having abolished in his flesh the enmity, even the law of commandments contained in ordinances; for to make in himself of twain one new man, so making peace.*

The Lord Jesus took His disciples inside and said, "I want to tell you a parable about one pearl of great price. Do not be so saddened to think that I am rejecting the Jews. I have this treasure hidden in a field. The field is the world. I will go to Calvary and purchase the whole field, the whole world." In the very next parable He turns and says, "I want to tell you about this one pearl of great price, which is not the Jew or the Gentile, but Jews and Gentiles who believe on the Lord Jesus Christ and make up His body, His church."

When the merchant man found that *"one pearl of great price,"* the Bible says He *"went and sold all that he had, and bought it."*

How did He buy it? He bought it with His own blood. The Bible says in I Corinthians 6:19-20, *"What? know ye not that your body is the temple of the Holy Ghost which is in you, which ye have of God, and ye are not your own? For ye are bought with a price: therefore glorify God in your body, and in your spirit, which are God's."*

*This parable of the one pearl of great price is about the Lord Jesus Christ purchasing the church with His own blood.*

The Bible says in Ephesians 5:24-25, *"Therefore as the church is subject unto Christ, so let the wives be to their own husbands in every thing. Husbands, love your wives, even as Christ also loved the church, and gave himself for it."*

This parable of the one pearl of great price is about the Lord Jesus Christ purchasing the church with His own blood. Why does He use the term *"pearl"*?

The word *"pearl"* is only found one time in the Old Testament, in the twenty-eighth chapter of Job. In the New Testament, the word *"pearl"* is used nine times. Two of those nine times it is used in this particular parable. But why did God choose the word *"pearl"*?

As we think about how pearls are formed and how the church was purchased, we understand the relationship. The Lord Jesus Christ chose the pearl to represent His work.

# A Pearl Comes From a Living Organism

The pearl is the only precious stone that comes from a living organism. One can mine a diamond. One can find emeralds. But a pearl comes from a living organism. It is embedded in an oyster, a living creature. Our living God came, was robed in flesh, and dwelt among us. This one pearl of great price begins with our living Savior.

# A Pearl Is Formed From Common, Lowly Material

A pearl is formed from common, lowly material, like a tiny grain of sand. That seems to be the most unsuspecting thing in the world to become a pearl. It embeds itself into the shell of the oyster and becomes an awful irritant, an intruder or offender. It finds its way inside the shell. It is the tiniest, most common thing. You could never imagine that something so common and lowly could become such a beautiful pearl.

When we think about our lives and what God has done with us and is going to do with us as a church, no one could ever imagine that God could take such lowly, common material and make anything so beautiful and grand as His church out of it; but He does.

# A Pearl Is a Product of Suffering and Death

When that tiny grain of sand is embedded in the shell of the oyster, the oyster begins to secrete a substance that really is the very life of the oyster. This substance is secreted from the oyster around the tiny grain of sand. As the oyster produces this substance, which is what we call mother-of-pearl, it is really the "life's blood" of the oyster that is being given out to form the pearl.

As the substance is secreted, it finds its way around this tiny grain of sand causing great suffering to the oyster. This suffering is not simply from the sand being in the shell, but from the very life of the oyster being given out as this substance is secreted to form the pearl. For this *"one pearl of great price,"* the church that Jesus Christ purchased, the Lord gave His life's blood on the cross. Finally, the oyster has its life taken as this substance is secreted to form a pearl.

## A Pearl Is Formed Over A Long Period of Time

A pearl is not made with one secretion or in one day. Neither is this *"one pearl of great price"* formed in a short period of time. All the body of Christ has not yet met together. Some have yet to become a part. Some have already gone to glory. Some are alive today. It takes a long period of time for this tiny grain of sand to become a pearl.

I thank God that the emphasis of the Bible is on the local church, but there are people whose faces we have never seen, whose names we do not know, whose voices we have never heard, who are part of the body of Christ. They have been born into God's family. Jew and Gentile will make up this body purchased by the very blood of Jesus Christ. He gave His all to buy this one pearl of great price.

## A Pearl Is Beautiful to Behold

Almost everyone has recognized the beauty of the pearl, but no one would have given a second thought to a tiny grain of sand. The Bible says when He is finally finished and He comes for us, we shall see Him as He is. We shall be made like the Lord Jesus. We are going to be presented to Him without spot or wrinkle, beautiful, as a bride fit for our glorious Savior, our heavenly Groom. Finally, when it is finished, what a beautiful sight to behold.

No wonder Christ took these disciples inside the house and told them this parable of the *"one pearl of great price,"* which is a picture of His church. He is the merchant man who gives Himself and sheds His blood to purchase this one pearl of great price. As we think about the way the pearl is formed, we understand that He is talking about what He did to redeem.

When I understand this parable, I want to be more of what Jesus Christ saved me to be. When my wife and I got married I said that I loved her, and I did love her. I was just a kid, but I loved her with all the capacity I had. She said she loved me.

*The more understanding we have of what Jesus Christ has done for this "one pearl of great price," the more we are going to love*

I said I loved her when I married her. But after all these years, I know in my heart that because of the way the Lord has worked in my life, I have a greater capacity to love her. I still say the same thing, but God has changed my capacity to care as I have grown in Him.

It is a shame that many say they are Christians and that they love the Lord, but they have not grown in their capacity to love the Lord as they should have grown. They have neglected the fellowship with Him that reveals something of what it costs to bring us to Him. The more understanding we have of what Jesus Christ has done for this *"one pearl of great price,"* the more we are going to love Him. The more I think of Calvary and what Christ did for me, the more I love Him and want to serve Him.

# A NET CAST INTO THE SEA

he parables of the kingdom are packaged closely together, and there are seven of them. The parable of the net cast into the sea is the seventh in these parables of the kingdom. The Bible says in Matthew 13:47-51,

*Again, the kingdom of heaven is like unto a net, that was cast into the sea, and gathered of every kind: which, when it was full, they drew to shore, and sat down, and gathered the good into vessels, but cast the bad away. So shall it be at the end of the world: the angels shall come forth, and sever the wicked from among the just, and shall cast them into the furnace of fire: there shall be wailing and gnashing of teeth. Jesus saith unto them, Have ye understood all these things? They say unto him, Yea, Lord.*

Of course, the desire of Christ was for His disciples to understand what He was saying. We read the response they gave, but we know they really did not understand. I think how much we are like them. We often think we understand when we really do not. The Lord continues working and instructing us until we get hold of the great truths that transform our lives.

> *There are many people in the world who say they are Christians and know how to talk like a Christian, but they are not necessarily born-again people.*

In verse forty-seven, the Lord Jesus says that the kingdom of heaven was like *"a net, that was cast into the sea."* I believe it would be a great help to us if we would gather together the things we have learned and move from these things we have learned to what I believe to be the proper interpretation of this seventh kingdom parable.

Christ begins these seven parables with the parable of the sower. In the parable of the sower, He talks about the seed being sown in different types of soil. He shows us that not all the soils are receptive to the seed, but we should sow the seed everywhere. Not everyone in the world is going to come to Christ, but it is our responsibility to tell everyone in all the world about the Lord Jesus Christ.

In verse twenty-four, the Bible says, *"The kingdom of heaven is like unto a man which sowed good seed in his field: but while men slept, his enemy came and sowed tares among the wheat."* He talked about the wheat and the tares growing in the same field. In professing Christendom, not everyone who claims to be a Christian is a Christian. There are many people in the world who say they are Christians and know how to talk like a Christian, but they are not necessarily born-again people.

Then the Bible says in verse thirty-one, *"The kingdom of heaven is like to a grain of mustard seed."* This grain of mustard seed grew into an unnatural plant, a tree. It became a shelter of the enemies of God. We can learn some great lessons about the work of the Devil in this parable.

The next parable speaks of the leaven hid in three measures of meal. Every time the word *"leaven"* is mentioned in the Bible, it refers to evil. It also refers to evil here, where a little leaven leavened the whole lump.

In the first four parables spoken to the disciples and the multitude, the Lord Jesus is talking about what the Devil is doing between Christ's First Coming and His Second Coming. Then He goes inside the house and gives a fifth parable about a treasure hid in the field. This treasure is Israel, God's chosen people.

The sixth parable is about one pearl of great price. This one pearl of great price is the church for which the Lord Jesus Christ gave Himself. This brings us to the seventh parable. The Bible says in verse forty-seven, *"Again, the kingdom of heaven is like unto a net, that was cast into the sea."*

Christ has taken His disciples into a house, and He is dealing with things to come. Remember, our Lord's disciples were Jewish followers. They were looking for a kingdom. In the parabolic teaching that He gave them, He explained to them that Israel was hidden in a field. They have been set aside for a time. He used the term *"the kingdom"* and showed them that this kingdom had been postponed. Christ bought the whole field, the field being the world. With His own blood He paid for the sin debt of all men. He is not finished with the Jew.

The parable of the one pearl of great price deals with the church. This entails God's program between His First Coming and His Second Coming. In the church, we do not have Jew or Gentile, but all who believe on the name of the Lord Jesus Christ become a part of His body. The local church is the great emphasis of the New Testament.

We have seen the Lord in the house, with His disciples, explaining to them God's work among the Jews and through the church. If we stopped there, something would be missing. If we find what is missing, I believe we will find the key to understanding this seventh parable.

> *The local church is the great emphasis of the New Testament.*

Remember that I Corinthians 10:32 helps us to rightly divide the Word of God. The Bible says, *"Give none offence, neither to the Jews, nor to the Gentiles, nor to the church of God."* When you read the Word of God, you should understand that God is either speaking to the Jew, speaking to the Gentile, or speaking to the church. These disappointed disciples have a rejected king, King Jesus; but He shall rule and reign on the throne of His father, David. The only throne David ever ruled on was an earthly throne. The Bible teaches a literal reign of Christ upon the earth for one thousand years. This will take place after the Tribulation period.

According to the Bible, the next thing to take place on God's calendar is the Rapture of the church. The Lord will come in the clouds to catch His bride away, and the church will be caught up to be with Him in the clouds. Paul explained this to the church at Thessalonica in I Thessalonians 4:13-18. Those who have died in Christ and their bodies have been buried will be resurrected and reunited in the air with Jesus Christ. Many will be alive when He comes and will be changed in a moment, in the twinkling of an eye, and will be caught up together with them in the clouds. Paul concludes this passage by saying in verse eighteen, *"Wherefore comfort one another with these words."*

At the conclusion of this church age, the church will be raptured as the Lord Jesus comes for His bride; but the world will not end. During the Tribulation period, which is a seven-year period of time, the church will be gone. You will not find the church on the earth. If you read the Revelation of Jesus Christ and come to the fourth chapter, you do not find the church on the earth. Heaven opens, and the church is caught up to be with the Lord.

If in our thinking we move to the Tribulation period and look at what is going on during the period of Tribulation after the church is gone, we will find Jews and Gentiles. The Lord has already dealt with the Jew and He has already dealt with the church, so I believe that in this seventh kingdom parable He is dealing with the Gentiles.

This was significant for His disciples because the Gentile rulers were ruling the world in their day. They were thinking, "Where is His kingdom? Where is His promise? Where is the throne of the Messiah? Has God failed? Has His program failed?"

At that time, Rome ruled the world; and before the Romans, the Greeks; and before the Greeks, the Medes and Persians; and before the Medes and Persians, the Babylonians. These were four great world empires. These were the times of the Gentiles and the scattering of the people of God. When will it all end?

There is going to come one great, final chapter when the world says, "We are going to show you what it is like to live without God. We are going to have our own way." That period of time is called the Tribulation. It is a definite seven-year period of time that takes place on the earth. At the conclusion of that seven years, Christ will come, His feet will touch the Mount of Olives, and the Mount of Olives will split. We refer to that literally as the Second Coming of Jesus Christ.

We may understand this better if we see that Christ's coming takes place in two phases. The first phase is the Rapture and the second phase is the Revelation of Jesus Christ. When He comes in the

Rapture and the church is caught up, only the church will hear the sound of the trumpet. Only the saved will be gone. This will mark the beginning of the Tribulation. When that Tribulation period concludes, and Jesus Christ comes in His revelation, every eye will see Him. Christ will establish His millennial kingdom on earth.

If we could take a little story, a parable, and try to explain what is going to happen to the Gentiles at the conclusion of the Tribulation period just before these Jews and their Messiah establish the kingdom they have always been looking for, then this seventh parable of the kingdom parables would be the story. This parable explains what is going to happen at the end of the Tribulation period.

I want you to think again of the parable in Matthew 13:47. The Bible says, *"Again, the kingdom of heaven is like unto a net, that was cast into the sea, and gathered of every kind..."*

Not all the same kind of fish were gathered. They were looking for good fish, but they had every kind of fish. Remember that a parable is a story cast alongside a great truth. The parable continues, *"...which, when it was full, they* [human instruments] *drew it to shore, and sat down, and gathered the good into vessels, but cast the bad away."* There was a time when the good were divided from the bad.

Let us compare Scripture with Scripture. God gives us a commentary on this parable in the twenty-fifth chapter of the Gospel according to Matthew. This part of the Olivet discourse does not deal with the Rapture but with the Tribulation period.

The Bible says in Matthew 25:31-32,

> *When the Son of man shall come in his glory, and all the holy angels with him, then shall he sit upon the throne of his glory: and before him shall be gathered all nations: and he shall separate them one from another, as a shepherd divideth his sheep from the goats.*

We believe that the word *"nations"* means "Gentiles." Some people think that the nations are going to come before the Lord. They think that all of Russia will be called up, all of America will be called up, and so on. But let us think about this as Gentiles; not a judgment of entire nations at one time, but of individuals. When God is talking here, He is talking about the Gentiles.

The Bible continues in verses thirty-three to forty-six,

> *And he shall set the sheep on his right hand, but the goats on his left. Then shall the King say unto them on his right hand, Come, ye blessed of my Father, inherit the kingdom prepared for you from the foundation of the world: for I was an hungred, and ye gave me meat: I was thirsty, and ye gave me drink: I was a stranger, and ye took me in: naked, and ye clothed me: I was sick, and ye visited me: I was in prison, and ye came unto me. Then shall the righteous answer him, saying, Lord, when saw we thee an hungred, and fed thee? or thirsty, and gave thee drink? When saw we thee a stranger, and took thee in? or naked, and clothed thee? Or when saw we thee sick, or in prison, and came unto thee? And the King shall answer and say unto them, Verily I say unto you, Inasmuch as ye have done it unto one of the least of these my brethren, ye have done it unto me.*

When He says *"my brethren"* He is not just talking about anyone. He is talking about the Jews.

> *Then shall he say also unto them on the left hand, Depart from me, ye cursed, into everlasting fire, prepared for the devil and his angels: for I was an hungred, and ye gave me no meat; I was thirsty, and ye gave me no drink: I was a stranger, and ye took me not in: naked, and ye clothed me not: sick, and in prison,*

*and ye visited me not. Then shall they also answer him, saying, Lord, when saw we thee an hungred, or athirst, or a stranger, or naked, or sick, or in prison, and did not minister unto thee? Then shall he answer them, saying, Verily I say unto you, Inasmuch as ye did it not to one of the least of these, ye did it not to me. And these shall go away into everlasting punishment: but the righteous into life eternal.*

You will never understand this passage until you get a grasp of the following statement: Works *prove* salvation; they do not *produce* salvation. It is very important that you understand this.

If we took this passage alone, and we got the idea that Gentile people were going to be saved because of the way they treated Jews during the Tribulation period, then we would have to find some way to prove that there is a way of salvation other than believing the gospel and believing on Jesus Christ. There is no other way.

These people respond to the Jews, not in order to be saved, but because they are saved. Works prove their salvation. Works do not produce their salvation. They prove they are saved by the way they respond to God's people and God's message.

In the seventh chapter of the Revelation of Jesus Christ, the church is gone from the earth. The Jew and the Gentile are still here. The Lord has told a parable about a net cast into the sea and all kinds of fish are caught in it. Human instrumentality is used to draw the net. They pull it to shore, signifying that the fishing is over. This shows the finality. The catch is in. There is a dividing of the fish–the good to the right, and the bad cast out to the left. The good are placed in vessels, and the bad are cast out.

A commentary on the same passage in Matthew 25 talks about the sheep and the goats. The Lord Jesus said, "You prove whether you are a sheep or a goat by the way you have treated My brethren."

What is actually going to happen during the Tribulation period? I do not understand it all. I am a little leery of anyone who says he does understand it all. I do know that Christ never told us to look for signs. He never told us to look for the Antichrist. He did tell us to look for Him, and I am looking for Him. I know that I am going to be caught up to be with Him and the Tribulation period is going to be ushered in. The restraining work of the Spirit of God is going to be removed. But there is going to be a great revival going on during the Tribulation period through 144,000 sealed, chosen Jews who preach the message of

> *Works prove salvation; they do not produce salvation.*

salvation. When they preach the message of salvation, an innumerable host of people are going to believe it and get saved. Not everyone will, but a great number will.

When the Lord comes in His revelation at the conclusion of that Tribulation period, the saved people, who have believed the message of those 144,000 flaming, Jewish evangelists are going to go into the millennial kingdom with Christ. He is going to sit on the throne that He did not sit on when He had those disciples in the house alone that day explaining to them His plan for the future.

The Bible says in Revelation 7:1-4,

> *And after these things I saw four angels standing on the four corners of the earth, holding the four winds of the earth, that the wind should not blow on the earth, nor on the sea, nor on any tree. And I saw another angel ascending from the east, having the seal of the living God: and he cried with a loud voice to the four angels, to whom it was given to hurt the earth and the sea, saying, Hurt not the earth, neither the sea, nor the trees, till we have sealed the servants*

> *of our God in their foreheads. And I heard the*
> *number of them which were sealed: and there were*
> *sealed an hundred and forty and four thousand of all*
> *the tribes of the children of Israel.*

He then talks about how many are sealed from each tribe. Then in verses nine through fourteen we read,

> *After this I beheld, and, lo, a great multitude,*
> *which no man could number, of all nations, and*
> *kindreds, and people, and tongues, stood before the*
> *throne, and before the Lamb, clothed with white*
> *robes, and palms in their hands; and cried with a*
> *loud voice, saying, Salvation to our God which sitteth*
> *upon the throne, and unto the Lamb. And all the*
> *angels stood round about the throne, and about the*
> *elders and the four beasts, and fell before the throne*
> *on their faces, and worshipped God, saying, Amen:*
> *Blessing, and glory, and wisdom, and thanksgiving,*
> *and honour, and power, and might, be unto our God*
> *for ever and ever. Amen. And one of the elders*
> *answered, saying unto me, What are these which are*
> *arrayed in white robes? and whence came they? And*
> *I said unto him, Sir, thou knowest. And he said to me,*
> *These are they which came out of great tribulation,*
> *and have washed their robes, and made them white in*
> *the blood of the Lamb.*

This is an innumerable host, people which no man could number. They are of all nations, and kindreds, and people, and tongues. They stood before the throne and before the Lamb. These were not wicked, not unrighteous, not goats, not bad fish, but saved people.

You may say, "I don't understand all of this." Go inside that house with the disciples and look at them. They said, "We understand all this," but they did not. The Lord told them before He ascended into heaven,

> *These things have I spoken unto you, being yet present with you. But the Comforter, which is the Holy Ghost, whom the Father will send in my name, he shall teach you all things, and bring all things to your remembrance, whatsoever I have said unto you* (John 14:25-26).

# GOD IS IN CONTROL

The apostle Paul was used of God to write and tell us that the Lord will illumine us and teach us His Word so that we will understand it. If you do not understand everything, that is all right. As we consider this parable, let us be sure to understand that God is in control.

To the disciples, it seemed as if God's plan was caving in. People not only rejected the Lord Jesus; they called Him the Devil. He came as Messiah. The disciples said, "We have found the Messiah, the promised Savior of the world."

Now He is going to Calvary to bleed and die, to deliver Himself into the hands of these Romans to be crucified. His disciples are going to see Him die; but this is God's plan. Jesus Christ came to suffer, bleed, and die. The disciples will read passages like Psalm 22 and Isaiah 53, and they will understand about a bleeding, suffering Savior. He came first to bleed and die.

Sometimes it may look as if the wicked are winning and God has been dethroned, but God is still in control. When the Lord Jesus took the disciples inside that house, He said, "Now I have you all alone here. I want to tell you about the Jews, about the church, and about the Gentiles. I want to tell you, there is going to be a kingdom some day." Do you get the idea that God is in control? This is one truth we need to get hold of.

## SALVATION IS IN JESUS CHRIST

As we have studied this parable, we have seen that salvation is only in Jesus Christ. There is no other way to be saved. God's Word says, *"Neither is there salvation in any other: for there is none other name under heaven given among men, whereby we must be saved"* (Acts 4:12). He is the only way of salvation.

In Revelation the question is asked, "Where do these come from, this innumerable host from all kindreds, tongues, and nations?" He said, "They came out of the Great Tribulation, and had their robes washed in the blood of the Lamb." Do you get the idea that salvation for all time is in Jesus Christ and Christ alone?

## GOD IS A GOD OF JUDGMENT

As we have looked at this parable, we have also seen that God is a God of judgment. People think they are going to get by, but they are not. God is a God of judgment. There is no doubt about it.

Sit with His disciples, this band of believers who followed the Lord from Galilee. Only one, Judas Iscariot, did not come from Galilee. Keep hearing the expression from Luke 24:21 ringing in your mind. It was after the death, burial, and resurrection of Christ, before they had seen the risen Lord, those disciples said, *"We trusted that it had been he which should have redeemed Israel."* The Lord Jesus explained the Word of God to these disciples and opened the Scriptures to them. Then they realized that it behooved Him to suffer and that this was all in God's plan.

Stand with those disciples in Jerusalem. This is not Rome. Look at the leaders of Israel. Look at these Jewish religious leaders; they have rejected Christ. They cry out, *"Crucify Him. We have no king but Caesar."* Then they are going to take Him, like a helpless, little lamb that has no power of His own, and make Him bleed and die. They are going to nail Him to a cross. The disciples are going to scatter like frightened children. It is going to seem as if the Gentiles have ruled the world, God is dethroned, and everything is wiped out. Then they are going to remember the story that He told them in the house that day.

> *Sometimes it may look as if the wicked are winning and God has been dethroned, but God is still in control.*

There is going to come a day when the Lord Jesus will judge the world. People say, "I can't understand it all." Let us just keep it simple. Do you get the idea that God really does have a program and a plan and He really is in control no matter what it might look like? People get worked up about presidents, programs, and peace plans; but we must realize that God is in control.

# Chapter Nine

# THE UNFORGIVING SERVANT

I n the eighteenth chapter of the Gospel of Matthew, the question of greatness is brought to the Lord Jesus. As the Lord deals with the subject of greatness, we find that greatness is related to forgiveness.

Greatness in the Christian life is demonstrated by our willingness to forgive. There is no greatness in the life of a Christian who is unforgiving. If you harbor unforgiveness in your life, then you are not the Christian God desires for you to be.

Our Lord spoke of how to keep things right in the church in part of this eighteenth chapter. After talking about trespassing and forgiving trespasses, the Bible says in verses twenty-one through thirty-five,

> *Then came Peter to him, and said, Lord, how oft*
> *shall my brother sin against me, and I forgive him?*
> *till seven times? Jesus saith unto him, I say not*

*unto thee, Until seven times: but, Until seventy times seven. Therefore is the kingdom of heaven likened unto a certain king, which would take account of his servants. And when he had begun to reckon, one was brought unto him, which owed him ten thousand talents. But forasmuch as he had not to pay, his lord commanded him to be sold, and his wife, and children, and all that he had, and payment to be made. The servant therefore fell down, and worshipped him, saying, Lord, have patience with me, and I will pay thee all. Then the lord of that servant was moved with compassion, and loosed him, and forgave him the debt. But the same servant went out, and found one of his fellowservants, which owed him an hundred pence: and he laid hands on him, and took him by the throat, saying, Pay me that thou owest. And his fellowservant fell down at this feet, and besought him, saying, Have patience with me, and I will pay thee all. And he would not: but went and cast him into prison, till he should pay the debt. So when his fellowservants saw what was done, they were very sorry, and came and told unto their lord all that was done. Then his lord, after that he had called him, said unto him, O thou wicked servant, I forgave thee all that debt, because thou desiredst me: shouldest not thou also have had compassion on thy fellowservant, even as I had pity on thee? And his lord was wroth, and delivered him to the tormentors, till he should pay all that was due unto him. So likewise shall my heavenly Father do also unto you, if ye from your hearts forgive not every one his brother their trespasses.*

What a story! Notice the beautiful expression, *"I forgave thee."* This is one of the most beautiful expressions in the Bible. Praise

God! We are forgiven. Our God desires to forgive. The goal of forgiveness is to bring us into right relationship and fellowship with Him. The Bible says, *"I forgave thee."*

Peter asked Christ the question in verse twenty-one, *"Lord, how oft shall my brother sin against me, and I forgive him?"*

He did not wait for an answer; instead, he answered it himself. This is much like all of us. Peter thought he had a good answer, and he said, *"Till seven times?"*

The idea of that day was that if someone sinned against you once, you would forgive him. If he sinned against you twice, it took much of the grace of God, but you should forgive him. If he sinned against you the third time, forget about it; forgiveness was over. Peter doubled this number and added one to it. After doubling it and adding one to it, he thought he was really something special. He said, "Lord, how about seven times? I will forgive him seven times." The Bible says, *"Jesus saith unto him, I say not unto thee, Until seven times: but, Until seventy times seven."*

> *Greatness in the Christian life is demonstrated by our willingness to forgive.*

If you are interested in multiplying seventy times seven and figuring out how many times it is, and somehow keeping a record of how many times you forgive, this is not what the Lord had in mind. What He had in mind was that we just keep on forgiving. Because He never runs out of forgiveness, we should never run out of forgiveness. When we think about how God has treated us and how often we have called on Him for forgiveness, we are well past seventy times seven. Because we have gone beyond seventy times seven with the Lord, we should be willing to go beyond seventy times seven in forgiving others.

How can we judge our development in the Christian life? Most Christians who are no longer growing in the Lord are stuck because they refuse to forgive. They are mired deeply in an unforgiving spirit, and God cannot bless them.

When we come to the end of this parable, we are going to find out about the tormentors. Many are tormented because of unforgiveness.

The Christian life is about being in right relationship with God. There are two words that we need to understand. The idea is not simply to know what the words mean, but to live them in our daily lives.

The first word is *relationship*. I must know that I am a child of God by relationship. I have been born into God's family. All of my sin has been forgiven. When I trusted Jesus Christ as my Savior, I believed on the Lord Jesus Christ who paid my debt and suffered my death and hell. No matter how much we owe, or how little we think we owe, as far as the sin debt is concerned, no one could ever fully pay for his sin. We have sinned against an infinite God, and we owe a debt we cannot pay.

God desires to bring us into right relationship with Him by forgiving all our sin, and seeing us as He sees His own dear Son, with no sin separating us in our relationship to God. When we ask God to forgive our sin and by faith trust Jesus Christ as our Savior, He imputes, or puts on our account, the righteousness of Jesus Christ. He counts that our sin debt was paid for on the cross when Jesus Christ died for our sins.

In Hebrews 10:17 the Bible says, *"And their sins and iniquities will I remember no more."* The Lord remembers to forget. This is unlike the human race. When God forgives, He forgets. He remembers our sin no more. When we forgive, it means that we do not bring them up any more. This is a hard thing to do. When people hurt us, we bury those memories in our minds. We will not give them to God and forgive. At some opportune time, which is usually the most inopportune time, we bring them up. This only proves that we have never forgiven.

However, in our relationship with God, the Bible says, *"Their sins and iniquities will I remember no more."*

When I was growing up, there was a period in my life when I seemed to be loose at both ends. I thought I was my own boss, and I had the idea that I could run my own life. My mother was only five feet tall and weighed one hundred pounds. I was much bigger than she, and I thought, "I can do as I please." I have regretted those thoughts.

When I was eighteen years old, I sat down and wrote a letter to my mother and said to her, "Mother, I know there were times in my life when I broke your heart. I did things that I should not have done, but I have made a promise to God that it will never happen again. I make a promise to you that as long as I live, from this day forward, I will make you glad to say that I am your son."

I have not lived a perfect life, but I have tried to live in such a way that I please God and honor my mother. That letter was a definite act of seeking her forgiveness, and getting it, and declaring that I wanted to do what was right. I was still her son. The *relationship* was never severed. I was her child, but the *fellowship* was not what it should have been.

This is the second word we need to know; not only our relationship with God, but our *fellowship* with God. Because God has forgiven our sins and remembers them no more, we can be in right relationship with God. There is never a time that sin comes between us and God in our relationship. It is gone, buried in the depths of the sea, removed as far as the east is from the west, cast behind God's back. The prophet said in Isaiah 38:17, *"Behold, for peace I had great bitterness: but thou hast in love to my soul delivered it from the pit of corruption: for thou hast cast all my sins behind thy back."*

Our sins are gone and will never be remembered again. My relationship is settled forever with God. I have been born into His family. I am one of His children. However, I need to work on my fellowship with Him. God has made a provision for our fellowship.

The Bible says in I John 1:5-10,

> *This then is the message which we have heard of him, and declare unto you, that God is light, and in him is no darkness at all. If we say that we have fellowship with him, and walk in darkness, we lie, and do not the truth: but if we walk in the light, as he is in the light, we have fellowship one with another, and the blood of Jesus Christ his Son cleanseth us from all sin. If we say that we have no sin, we deceive ourselves, and the truth is not in us. If we confess our sins, he is faithful and just to forgive us our sins, and to cleanse us from all unrighteousness. If we say that we have not sinned, we make him a liar, and his word is not in us.*

To confess our sins is to agree with God. As we agree with God that we have sinned, He will forgive us. He is faithful and just. You may say, "How can God forgive sin? How can He be just in doing it? The debt is owed." No, the debt is not owed. The debt has been paid in the blood of the Lord Jesus. This is how He can be just in forgiving us.

The Bible says, *"He is faithful and just to forgive us our sin…"* This is forgiveness. *"…and to cleanse us from all unrighteousness."* He not only takes care of the sin, He takes care of the guilt. He deals with our fellowship.

You can be married to a lovely lady and have a relationship with her. As far as your marriage is concerned, you call her your wife and she calls you her husband. But the truth of the matter is, you can have a relationship and not have fellowship.

You can be a father or mother. Your children can call you their mom and dad. You have a relationship that can never be severed, but the fellowship can be terrible. Fellowship means that we agree on things. We fellowship or come together on points of agreement. This is the sweet, precious thing about a church family. We can have wonderful fellowship because of what Christ has done in our lives.

In this parable, our Lord helps Peter and other followers with this clear teaching. He says in verses twenty-three and twenty-four, *"Therefore is the kingdom of heaven likened unto a certain king..."*

I believe this king represents to us God, our heavenly Father. *"...which would take account of his servants. And when he had begun to reckon, one was brought unto him, which owed him ten thousand talents."*

## A Debt That Could Not Be Paid

Ten thousand talents would be equivalent to millions and millions of dollars. In other words, this king had a servant who owed him untold millions of dollars. There was absolutely nothing that this servant could ever do to repay such a debt. It was beyond repaying. And so, as the accounting was done, the Bible says in Matthew 18:25-27,

> *But forasmuch as he had not to pay, his lord commanded him to be sold, and his wife, and children, and all that he had, and payment to be made. The servant therefore fell down, and worshipped him, saying, Lord, have patience with me, and I will pay thee all. Then the lord of that servant was moved with compassion, and loosed him, and forgave him the debt.*

He was to be sold. His wife was to be sold. His children were to be sold. Everything he had was to be sold. In other words, he had absolutely nothing.

# HIS DEBT WAS FORGIVEN

Notice that the indebted servant, who owed millions, said, "Please be patient with me, and I will pay thee the debt." But the lord had compassion toward this servant. He did not make arrangements for the servant to pay the debt; he simply forgave the debt.

> *To confess our sins is to agree with God. As we agree with God that we have sinned, He will forgive us. He is faithful and just.*

I hope by now you can see that this lord is our Lord, and this servant is each of us as sinners. We owe a debt we cannot pay, but God in mercy, love, and compassion forgives us.

Peter said to the Lord Jesus, "When I am trespassed against, how often should I forgive?" All of us who are Christians should see ourselves here. We should see that we have been forgiven by the Lord of the great sin debt we owed. God simply forgave us. He was just in forgiving us because His own dear Son paid our sin debt for us.

# THE UNFORGIVENESS OF THE FORGIVEN

As we continue in this parable, we are not going to deal with the servant and his lord; we are going to deal with the servant and other servants. What we are doing in this parable is moving from our relationship with God to our relationship with other people. It is quite simple. As a matter of fact, this is one of the simplest parables to understand; but it is perhaps the most difficult parable to practice.

The Bible says in verse twenty-eight, *"But the same servant went out, and found one of his fellowservants, which owed him an hundred pence: and he laid hands on him, and took him by the throat, saying, Pay me that thou owest."*

The hundred pence was just a few dollars compared to the ten thousand talents. So, in comparison, what the servant owed his fellowservant was absolutely nothing compared to what the servant owed his lord. This is easy for us to understand. What other people owe us is no comparison to the debt we owed God, yet God forgave us.

However, for a few measly dollars, the servant who had been forgiven of millions of dollars worth of debt would not forgive his fellowservant. The Bible continues this story by saying in verse twenty-nine, *"And his fellowservant fell down at his feet, and besought him, saying, Have patience with me, and I will pay thee all."*

This sounds like the same speech the other servant had made to his lord. The only difference is that his lord heard him and had compassion.

Verses thirty and thirty-one tell us, *"And he would not: but went and cast him into prison, till he should pay the debt. So when his fellowservants saw what was done, they were very sorry, and came and told unto their lord all that was done."*

## UNFORGIVENESS AFFECTS MANY OTHERS

This unforgiveness between servants disrupted fellowship with all the servants. Dear friends, any unforgiveness among the servants disrupts all the other servants. Do you want to tear your wonderful church to pieces? All you have to do is harbor unforgiveness in your heart toward someone else. This is the most serious matter that could ever be dealt with in the heart of a church. Unforgiveness not only destroys the life of the holder, it destroys families and friendships also.

Do not allow unforgiveness in your heart. You cannot have that feeling toward someone without it affecting the whole fellowship. You may be on your way to the tormentors and do not know it. May God help us. We have been there in our homes. We have been there in our churches. We have been there on our jobs.

# UNFORGIVENESS IS WICKED

The Bible continues the story in Matthew 18:32-33,

> *Then his lord, after that he had called him, said unto him, O thou wicked servant, I forgave thee all that debt, because thou desiredst me: shouldest not thou also have had compassion on thy fellowservant, even as I had pity on thee?*

The Lord says to us, *"I forgave thee."* The point is that forgiven people should be quick to forgive others. We have either forgotten that we have been forgiven, or we have gotten so far from our fellowship with God that His forgiveness does not mean to us what it should mean to us.

The Bible says in verses thirty-four and thirty-five,

> *And his lord was wroth, and delivered him to the tormentors, till he should pay all that was due unto him. So likewise shall my heavenly Father do also unto you, if ye from your hearts forgive not every one his brother their trespasses.*

It is enough for someone who has trespassed against you to say, "I repent." You should forgive him. But it is not enough for you to say, "I forgive," and not do it from your heart. How is your heart in this matter of forgiveness?

When we will not forgive, we grieve the Lord. In Ephesians 4:30-32 the Bible says,

> *And grieve not the holy Spirit of God, whereby ye are sealed unto the day of redemption. Let all bitterness, and wrath, and anger, and clamour, and evil speaking, be put away from you, with all malice: and be ye kind one to another, tenderhearted, forgiving one another, even as God for Christ's sake hath forgiven you.*

God did not forgive us for our sake. He forgave us for Christ's sake. Some may say, "I have been repentant. I have come to God in sackcloth and ashes. I have said, 'O Lord, I am so sorry for my sins. Dear God, I wish I had never done it. O Lord, I have made such a terrible mistake. Dear God, I brought such shame and disgrace. You see how sorry I am. You see how much I need forgiveness.'" God does not forgive us because of this. He forgives us for Christ's sake.

*You cannot have a happy home until you forgive.*

We can cry out to God all we want to, but He could and would not hear us had not Jesus Christ paid the debt so that God could be just in forgiving us.

The Devil wants to get a wedge between you and the people you love most in life. He will try to use unforgiveness to do this. Some of you could have a happy home if you would forgive. You cannot have a happy home until you forgive. Unforgiveness is like slamming the door and saying, "Don't ever come back into my life." It is like telling that prodigal son, "You die out there in the hog pen. I don't want to see you again." That is the way people treat their children and their mates when they refuse to forgive. It is wicked not to forgive.

When we are tempted to be unforgiving, we should think of Calvary. Think of the debt we owed that we could not pay, and in compassion God forgave us all.

Unforgiveness can happen in the church. People in the church get irritated with other people. I have been in churches where family members sat on different sides of the building. They had been there for twenty years and would not speak to one another. They made sure they came in and went out different doors so they did not have to talk to one another. This means that for all those years they had not been able to talk to God either. Do you know where they had been? They had been to the tormentors.

One of these day they are going to go to a graveside. Someone they love is going to be buried, and they are going to cry at the funeral service because they left things unresolved. If they are saved, they are going to get to the judgment seat of Christ and lose reward. If they are not saved, they are going to go to hell and find out that it was not worth holding on to. We need to forgive.

*Think of the debt we owed that we could not pay, and in compassion God forgave us all.*

Peter was told by the Lord in the eighteenth chapter, "You are going to have offenses. Offenses will come. It is part of life." Sometimes when these offenses come, we simply want to retaliate. We want to be mean to people who are mean to us, or we want to be mean to people who are mean to the people we love. It is in our old nature to be that way. How do we hold back? We must think of Christ. Calvary captures us. We need to think about how we have been forgiven and how we should forgive others. We must realize that God forgives us for Christ's sake. We must think of Calvary, and what the Lord has done for us. The Bible says, *"I forgave thee."* That is enough–forgive others!

# LABORERS IN THE VINEYARD

n the first sixteen verses of Matthew chapter twenty, our Lord gives a parable in answer to a question asked by the apostle Peter. This parable is not about salvation, but about service.

Peter, along with the other disciples, had been watching as Christ talked to a young man we call the rich young ruler. The young man evidently had many worldly possessions but came to Christ and asked in Matthew 19:16, *"Good Master, what good thing shall I do, that I may have eternal life?"* The Lord Jesus said to him, *"There is none good but one, that is, God"* (Matthew 19:17).

In this statement, the Lord Jesus declared to this inquirer that if he were calling Christ good, *"There is none good but God,"* he was recognizing that Christ is God. If so, he should be willing to do anything God wanted him to do.

The moment a man realizes there is a God, he should be on his knees somewhere saying, "What is it God wants me to do?"

Christ talked to the young man. In one account the Bible says he was very wealthy. Remember that the disciples were watching all of this. The Word of God says that he walked away from Christ *"sorrowful."*

When the Lord returned to His disciples, they were thinking, "We have forsaken everything we have and followed Him. This fellow gets to keep everything he has."

Their spokesperson, Peter, questioned Christ. The Bible says in Matthew 19:27-30,

> *Then answered Peter and said unto him, Behold, we have forsaken all, and followed thee; what shall we have therefore? And Jesus said unto them, Verily I say unto you, That ye which have followed me, in the regeneration when the Son of man shall sit in the throne of his glory, ye also shall sit upon twelve thrones, judging the twelve tribes of Israel. And every one that hath forsaken houses, or brethren, or sisters, or father, or mother, or wife, or children, or lands, for my name's sake, shall receive an hundredfold, and shall inherit everlasting life. But many that are first shall be last; and the last shall be first.*

When the disciples saw this young man walk away keeping everything he had, they said, *"We have forsaken all, and followed thee; what shall we have therefore?"* The Lord spoke to them. He talked to them about forsaking things that they loved–houses, lands, and family members. He talked to them about their reward–an hundredfold in this life, and after this life, life everlasting.

A great principle was established here for followers of the Lord. We are called upon as Christians to give up something or someone we love, for Someone we are to love more. Following the Lord Jesus Christ is forsaking something that you love for Someone you love more.

How can a young couple with babies in arms leave their homeland and travel somewhere thousands of miles across the sea, kissing parents and grandparents goodbye? How can they choose to live in much less desirable circumstances than they could or would live in at home? What is it that causes Christian people to be willing to do this? They can do this because they have come to know the Lord Jesus Christ and have grown to love Him so much that they love Him more than they love other people and things. They are willing to leave land, houses, family, and friends, not because they do not love those people and love those things, but because they love Christ more.

Can I truthfully say that I would be willing to do anything and go anywhere God leads? This is a matter of heart searching we each must do. Unless we have yielded in this way to the Lord, we cannot expect His blessing.

The Lord Jesus had answered the disciples' question in this parable by saying, *"Whatsoever is right I will give you."*

This parable is a story of a man who had a big job to do. He went down to a place where he could hire laborers. The first group he approached said, "We will work for you, but we are not going to go until we have agreed on what we will be paid." Perhaps out of the corner of His eye, Christ caught Peter's glance, because Peter had spoken for all the disciples in saying, *"What shall we have therefore?"* The first group in this parable would not go work for the man who needed laborers until the man was specific about what he would pay them.

The Bible says in Matthew 20:1-2, *"For the kingdom of heaven is like unto a man that is an householder, which went out early in the morning to hire labourers into his vineyard. And when he had agreed with the labourers for a penny a day, he sent them into his vineyard."*

What kind of pastor would you think I was if I sat down with a pulpit committee of a church and said, "Before I can tell you that I am going to come to your church, I want to know what kind of salary I am going to get, what kind of benefits I am going to have, and how much time I am going to have off"? That may make sense in the business world, but I guarantee you a spiritually-minded church looking for a pastor does not want to hear that kind of thing. They get the idea, if a man talks like that, he is more concerned about what is in it for him than he is about pleasing the Lord and following Christ by faith.

*Following the Lord Jesus Christ is forsaking something that you love for Someone you love more.*

These laborers said, "We are not going to go until we have agreed." The Jewish day started at six in the morning. There were twelve hours in the day. The first hour of the day was seven o'clock; the second hour was eight o'clock; the third hour was nine o'clock; the fourth hour was ten o'clock; the fifth hour was eleven o'clock; the sixth hour of the day was at noon; the seventh hour was at one; the eighth hour was at two; the ninth hour was at three; the tenth hour was at four; the eleventh hour was at five; and the twelfth hour was at six.

The goodman went out early in the morning and said, "Let's go to work." They replied, "We want to work, but we must know what we are going to get." In verses three and four the Bible says, *"And he went out about the third hour, and saw others standing idle in the marketplace, and said unto them; Go ye also into the vineyard, and whatsoever is right I will give you."* This was about nine o'clock in the morning. There was no agreement made here. They just went.

In verse five the Bible says, *"Again he went out about the sixth and ninth hour, and did likewise."* This means He went out at noon and at three and did the same thing. No agreement was made. The laborers just went out, and He told them He would pay whatever was right. In verse six the Bible says, *"And about the eleventh hour he went out, and found others standing idle, and saith unto them, Why stand ye here all the day idle?"* They had been out there all day long doing nothing. Now only one hour was left to work.

> *They say unto him, Because no man hath hired us. He saith unto them, Go ye also into the vineyard; and whatsoever is right, that shall ye receive. So when even was come, the lord of the vineyard saith unto his steward, Call the labourers, and give them their hire, beginning from the last unto the first. And when they came that were hired about the eleventh hour, they received every man a penny. But when the first came, they supposed that they should have received more; and they likewise received every man a penny. And when they had received it, they murmured against the goodman of the house, saying, These last have wrought but one hour, and thou hast made them equal unto us, which have borne the burden and heat of the day. But he answered one of them, and said, Friend, I do thee no wrong: didst not thou agree with me for a penny? Take that thine is, and go thy way: I will give unto this last, even as unto thee. Is it not lawful for me to do what I will with mine own? Is thine eye evil, because I am good? So the last shall be first, and the first last: for many be called, but few chosen* (Matthew 20:7-16).

Notice the word *"supposed "* in verse ten. We get in so much trouble with our presumptuous sins and ideas. We all expect so much, but we are willing to give so little. I was thinking recently about big things and little things, and I thought about how people make the biggest fuss out of the smallest, most insignificant things.

Little or no consideration is given to the truly big things in life. Because of this, people blow up about the smallest of things. They give no consideration at all to what matters most in life.

At the end of the day, all the laborers got paid. The last crowd to get paid was the first crowd that went out. They had agreed on their wages before they ever went to work, or they would not have gone.

*We all expect so much, but we are willing to give so little.*

Watching others receive their wages, they became disgusted and outraged. They murmured about what they were paid, yet they would not go to work until they had agreed for that exact amount.

At this moment I think the Lord looked at His disciples. The question did not even need to be asked. If they really believed what they said they believed about the Lord, they should never have asked, *"What shall we have therefore?"* Christ can be trusted to care for His own.

My wife and I reared two boys. They asked many questions. They would have worried me absolutely to death if they had asked me every day, "What are you going to do for us today? Is there anything to eat in the house today? Is there a place for us to sleep tonight? Will we have a roof over our heads tonight?" Surely, if a failing father such as I can try to provide for a wife and two sons, then our heavenly Father can surely care for His children.

In Matthew 6:31-34 the Bible says,

> *Therefore take no thought, saying, What shall we eat? or, What shall we drink? or, Wherewithal shall we be clothed? (For after all these things do the Gentiles seek:) for your heavenly Father knoweth that ye have need of all these things. But seek ye first the kingdom of God, and his righteousness; and all*

*these things shall be added unto you. Take therefore
no thought for the morrow: for the morrow shall take
thought for the things of itself. Sufficient unto the day
is the evil thereof.*

We should note the expression, *"Your heavenly Father knoweth
that ye have need of all these things."*

There are times in life when it seems that every brook has dried
up, every barrel is empty, and every bill is due. We are rearing
children who need to know there is a great God who can meet our
needs. God allows us to get into situations where we cannot make it
without Him. For some it is not finances; it is something that seems
impossible to conquer, someone who is impossible to deal with, or
something that just will not work out the way it should work out. Our
children are watching. They need to learn that we are people of faith
in Christ who believe that our God can take care of all these things.

The disciples saw this rich young man walk away sorrowfully. If
you think he was sorrowful that day, think of him one moment after
he died knowing he had traded the world for Jesus Christ. Then he
would have given all the world for Christ. Instead, he kept the world
and traded Christ away.

## LABORERS ARE NEEDED

In this parable, the householder needed laborers in order to bring
in his harvest. Jesus Christ was filled with emotion as He stopped
His disciples one day and said, *"Pray ye therefore the Lord of the
harvest, that he will send forth labourers into his harvest"* (Matthew
9:38). In every nation of the world, people need Jesus Christ. In
every state in our nation, people need Jesus Christ. In every county
in our state, people need Jesus Christ. Down every street and in
every house, people need Jesus Christ.

How does the Lord get His message to people? People who have heard about Jesus Christ tell those who have not heard. Laborers are needed. If we are ever going to serve the Lord, we must do it now. We have so little time left in which to do it.

Think of what could be done if our churches moved like a mighty army with love for Christ and a passion for souls. Laborers are needed.

Are we going to be like the people who said, "Wait a minute. I will serve, but not until everything is worked out"? Or are we going to be like the crowd that said, "Lord, You just tell me. I am going to believe You"?

## LOOKING AT OTHERS WILL RUIN YOUR LIFE

If you have a serious problem in your life right now, perhaps a big part of it is that you have been watching someone else too closely. One of the things that we learn first in life is how disappointing people can be. The fastest way to go blind is to take your eyes off Jesus Christ.

Watching other people will ruin your life. These workers in the parable were watching everyone get paid. They looked at the first group and said, "See what they received." Then they looked at the second group and said, "See what they received." They looked at the third group and said, "See what they received."

The Lord has designed the Christian life so that we do not watch everyone else and listen to everyone else. If we do, we will stay upset all the time. The Lord has designed the Christian life so that we keep our eyes on Him. Hebrews 12:2 says, *"Looking unto Jesus the author and finisher of our faith."* Let us be laborers in the work of the Lord and keep our eyes *"looking unto Jesus"* as we serve Him.

# THE LORD IS TRUSTWORTHY

Every parable has one great point. The great point of this parable is that the Lord is trustworthy. In other words, Jesus Christ was saying, "Peter, can't you trust Me?" The Lord said, *"Whatsoever is right I will give you."* By the way, we do not decide what is right; He does. If we will let God do the deciding, He will decide much more in our favor than we ever imagined.

There is a precious promise given to us in Romans 8:32. The Bible says, *"He that spared not his own Son, but delivered him up for us all, how shall he not with him also freely give us all things?"*

Do we need to ask if God will provide when He has already provided His own Son? He gave the best. He gave all first. After that, there are no questions to ask. If our heavenly Father gave us the Lord Jesus, will He not freely give us all things? He has already proven that there is nothing He would not give us because He gave us His Son.

*The fastest way to go blind is to take your eyes off Jesus Christ.*

I can watch that scene unfold in my mind. I did not stand there with those disciples that day. I did not see that rich young ruler walk away with a sorrowful countenance after he talked to Christ. I did not see him keep everything. I did not stand there with that crowd and prod Peter to ask the question; but I have gone through life watching other people, thinking about what they had, what they did, and where they were. I have thought about how everything fell into their hands.

Do you know what I am thinking? I am thinking just as you think. I should be thanking God that He provides for me, that I have eaten today, that I have clothes on my back, a roof over my head, people who care for me, a family that loves me, and a God in heaven who has redeemed me. May God help us to have a great faith in God. We simply need to trust Him. He is trustworthy.

# THE TWO SONS
# CALLED TO WORK

As a teenager, I came to know the Lord Jesus Christ as my Savior. Since yielding my life to serve Him, I have come to believe that serving Christ is not an option. God intends for all of His children to serve Him.

In Matthew chapter twenty-one, we find a parable that the Lord Jesus gave in a very important context. He had made His triumphal entry into the city of Jerusalem. The people had cried out, *"Hosanna to the son of David."* It had caused quite a stir among the chief priests and religious leaders of the day. The Bible says in Matthew 21:28-32,

> *But what think ye? A certain man had two sons; and he came to the first, and said, Son, go work to day in my vineyard. He answered and said, I will not: but afterward he repented, and went. And he came to the second, and said likewise. And he answered and*

*said, I go, sir: and went not. Whether of them twain did the will of his father? They say unto him, The first. Jesus saith unto them, Verily I say unto you, That the publicans and the harlots go into the kingdom of God before you. For John came unto you in the way of righteousness, and ye believed him not: but the publicans and the harlots believed him: and ye, when ye had seen it, repented not afterward, that ye might believe him.*

Christ said to them, *"The publicans and the harlots believed him."* The publicans were a group of Jews who had sold out to the Roman

> *God intends for all of His children to serve Him.*

government. They were tax collectors. Israel was under the yoke of Roman bondage, and they hated the fact that they were under Roman rule. They wanted no foreign rule over them. It was a terrible thing in the eyes of the Jews for one of their own to sell out his people and work for these oppressive Romans as a tax collector. These tax collectors were referred to as publicans. The harlots were prostitutes. They were wicked women who sold their bodies into sin.

The Lord declared to these religious leaders, when speaking of the kingdom of God, that the publicans and the harlots would go into the kingdom of God before them. He also said that the publicans and the harlots believed Him.

In Matthew 21:12 the Bible says, *"And Jesus went into the temple of God, and cast out all them that sold and bought in the temple, and overthrew the tables of the moneychangers, and the seats of them that sold doves."*

Quite a stir had been made. Christ had made His triumphal entry. He had come to the temple mount. He had entered into the area where the moneychangers were busy working, and He turned their tables upside down, casting them out and declaring in verse thirteen, *"It is written, My house shall be called the house of prayer; but ye have made it a den of thieves."*

God's Word continues in verses fourteen and fifteen,

> *And the blind and the lame came to him in the temple; and he healed them. And when the chief priests and scribes saw the wonderful things that he did, and the children crying in the temple, and saying, Hosanna to the son of David; they were sore displeased.*

It is interesting to note two expressions in verse fifteen. The first is the expression *"wonderful things."* The second is the expression *"sore displeased."* It is hard to imagine that wonderful things were happening, and yet there were so many people who were sore displeased. Can you imagine something so marvelous taking place and people being *"sore displeased"* over it?

Many times, even among Christians, when God is blessing, souls are being saved, a mighty work is being done, and the Spirit of God is moving in people's lives, someone gets upset about something and is *"sore displeased."* We must guard our attitude all the time, but especially in the time when the Lord is doing something great among us. The Devil is looking for any opportunity to get in. The Bible says in verses sixteen and seventeen,

> *And said unto him, Hearest thou what these say? And Jesus saith unto them, Yea; have ye never read, Out of the mouth of babes and sucklings thou hast perfected praise? And he left them, and went out of the city into Bethany; and he lodged there.*

Later, Christ returns to Jerusalem. Matthew 21:23-27 says,

> *And when he was come into the temple, the chief priests and the elders of the people came unto him as*

*he was teaching, and said, By what authority doest thou these things? and who gave thee this authority? And Jesus answered and said unto them, I also will ask you one thing, which if ye tell me, I in like wise will tell you by what authority I do these things. The baptism of John, whence was it? from heaven, or of men? And they reasoned with themselves, saying, If we shall say, From heaven; he will say unto us, Why did ye not then believe him? But if we shall say, Of men; we fear the people; for all hold John as a prophet. And they answered Jesus, and said, We cannot tell. And he said unto them, Neither tell I you by what authority I do these things.*

They said to Him, "Who do you think You are, and by what authority are You coming in here and taking over?" The Lord Jesus said, "Before I answer your question, you answer one for Me." John the Baptist came preaching the Word of God. John the Baptist came declaring that Jesus Christ was the promised Messiah. They knew that. He said, "What do you think about John the Baptist's message?" They thought, "If we say that we believe that John the Baptist got his authority from God, then we should believe on this Jesus of Nazareth, whom John the Baptist declared to be the promised Messiah." We cannot say we believe he had authority from God, but if we say that he did not get his authority from God, we fear the people because many people believed John the Baptist. We are stuck." So they said, "We do not know the answer to that." They took the coward's way out.

*We must guard our attitude all the time, but especially in the time when the Lord is doing something great among us.*

Someone is going to say you are rude, unloving, or unkind when you speak up about what you believe, but if you ever intend to speak up, now is the time to do it. Do not be a coward about it.

When Christ received their response, He replied to them, saying, *"Neither tell I you by what authority I do these things."* Then, He told them this parable.

Christ had confronted the religious leaders with the preaching of John the Baptist. They would not say whether John the Baptist was preaching by the authority of God or not. The Lord Jesus had also come to the temple and had cleaned out the moneychangers and a number of religious leaders. As we look at this context, we feel the sting of this parable.

He says in Matthew 21:28-32,

> *But what think ye? A certain man had two sons; and he came to the first, and said, Son, go work today in my vineyard. He answered and said, I will not: but afterward he repented, and went. And he came to the second, and said likewise. And he answered and said, I go, sir: and went not. Whether of them twain did the will of his father? They say unto him, The first. Jesus saith unto them, Verily I say unto you, That the publicans and the harlots go into the kingdom of God before you. For John came unto you in the way of righteousness, and ye believed him not: but the publicans and the harlots believed him: and ye, when ye had seen it, repented not afterward, that ye might believe him.*

This is one of those parables in which the Lord places Himself. He is that *"certain man."*

The first son, when he was told to go work in the vineyard said, "I am not going to go." But the Bible says that he repented later and went.

The second son said he was going to go, but he did not go. He said he was obedient, but he was not obedient. He said he was going to please his father, but he did not please him. The question Christ asks is easy to answer. He says, *"Whether of them twain did the will of his father?"*

These religious leaders were very proud. They had not answered His first question, but they were ready to answer this one. They said, *"The first."* Then the Lord Jesus said unto them, *"Verily I say unto you, That the publicans and the harlots go into the kingdom of God before you."*

> *If you ever intend to speak up about what you believe, now is the time to do it.*

He was saying, "Here you are standing at the door of the kingdom of God. You have been given the responsibility to point people to God. You are keepers of the message of the kingdom of God. You are supposed to be the closest people on earth to the kingdom of God, but the people you despise most, the publicans and the harlots, go in before you."

This is like taking the most responsible, most admired church members, and bringing them in front of a public meeting and saying, "I want you to know something. Publicans and harlots, people on the streets who have sold their bodies into sin, are going to get to God before these get to God." He continues by saying, *"John came unto you in the way of righteousness, and ye believed him not: but the publicans and the harlots believed him: and ye, when ye had seen it, repented not afterward, that ye might believe him."*

He said, "John the Baptist came preaching the truth, and you pretended that you were following and obeying God. You are like that son who said, 'I will go,' but did not go. John the Baptist came preaching the truth, thundering forth the message of the righteousness of God, and when the publicans and harlots heard it they said, 'We will not.' Then under conviction of the Spirit of God, they repented and trusted the Lord. When you saw the mighty work of repentance that God was doing and how the Lord was moving and working, you still would not believe John's message and repent."

He was saying, "The first son, the obedient son, who said he would not go and then went, is like the publicans and harlots. The fellow who was all puffed up with himself and played the game and said, 'Yes, sir, I'll go,' but did not go, was wicked in his response because he pretended to be something that he wasn't. He is like you."

We have a Savior who speaks the truth and calls sin by name where He finds it. His Word pierces us and pricks our hearts. Who are we like? Are we like the people who are pretending to do what God wants? Are we pretending, just doing the motions of the work of the Lord, or are we actually doing the work of the Lord? There are people who grow up around Christianity and take it for granted. It is no longer real to them. We can actually envy these old, hardened sinners who come in and hear the gospel. They have rejected the Lord, but they hear the message of the saving grace of Jesus Christ and come running to the Savior for salvation full and free. We need to be very careful that we do not become cold and indifferent and hardened while we are seeing others who have lived lives of sin come to the Lord and trust Him, live for Him, and serve Him.

## AN UNFINISHED WORK

The Bible says in verse twenty-eight, *"But what ye think ye? A certain man had two sons; and he came to the first, and said, Son, go work to day in my vineyard."*

We are to do the Lord's work. He said, *"Go work to day in my vineyard."* This is an unfinished work. It is not completed yet. In every generation, God has given believers a work to do. They have the responsibility to witness and to evangelize their generation.

Finally, the last person is going to get saved and complete the bride of Christ, and the Lord Jesus Christ will come again.

People around us everywhere need to hear about Jesus Christ. We live in a world of over six billion people. This statistic staggers my mind. Over half the world's population has never heard the name of Jesus Christ in association with salvation. One fourth of the world's population, we are told, has heard about the Lord Jesus Christ but has never trusted Him as Savior. They make no claim to identify as any kind of Christian. About one fourth of the world's population claims to be Christian, but many of them are only Christian in name, because they have not trusted in the Lord Jesus Christ for salvation. Think how many people in this world still need the Lord. This is an unfinished work.

> *We have a Savior who speaks the truth and calls sin by name where He finds it. His Word pierces us and pricks our hearts.*

In America, more people do not go to church than people who do. Many areas are full of liberal churches that are not preaching the truth. The need is so great. This is an unfinished work.

Our Lord says, *"Go work."* This is a time to work. Everyone who says he knows the Lord should be working for the Lord. It is not enough to say, "Yes, sir, I'll go," and then sit and do nothing. Think how many people attend church services, listen to the preaching, sing the songs, and yet never teach a Sunday School class, never pray for the meetings, never witness to a soul, never give out a gospel tract, never bring anyone to church, and never seek to win anyone to Christ. How long has it been since some of us worked hard to get someone to church, to get someone saved? It is an unfinished work.

When I was a boy, on occasion, my mother would scold me because I would not get something done in the house while she was gone. She would say, "Why didn't you do this?" I would answer, "I didn't know it needed to be done." She would respond, "Can't you see everything that needs to be done right under your feet? Can't you see all that needs to be accomplished?" Oh, Christian friend, there is much to do for Christ right under our feet.

We need a moving of the Spirit of God in our own lives. This moving is not a condemning attitude about people outside of the church, but first and foremost a judging of our own selves. Judgment must begin at the house of God. We need to realize that God's work is an unfinished work, and all of us need to be laboring in His work.

## An Urgent Work

The father said, *"Go...to day."* There are two parts to this idea of doing the work today. One idea has to do with the passing of the harvest, the perishing of people all around us. If we do not do the work urgently, many will die before we ever get to work. A part of this urgency has to do with the harvest, but another great part of this urgency has to do with the laborer. Think of the difference it would make in our lives if we had the attitude that we are to do God's work urgently. We should do what needs to be done now. We must not procrastinate.

> *Everyone who says he knows the Lord should be working for the Lord.*

Often people say to me, "I do not know where my time goes. I do not have the time to do what I would like to do." What do you do with your time? Do you watch two or three hours of television a week or a day? There is not one person who could not take a three- or four-hour block of time and say, "I am going to give it all to God." May such an urgency come upon us that we will stop things of lesser importance and start giving time to things of most importance.

Is there an urgency in our lives about serving the Lord? I get disturbed thinking about how frivolous the world is about the things of God. Then I think about how God's people get so frivolous. You may say, "Are we to have no recreation? Are we to do nothing?" How much recreation do we need? How much entertainment do we need? How many hours do we need?

This is an urgent work. He said, *"Son, go work to day."* We should be "out of breath" for God. We need to let the Holy Spirit deal with us. We should let Him search our lives, our calendars, our appointments, and our days. We should let the Lord say to us, "Give Me those hours. Give Me that part of the day. Give Me that time."

The average American watches five hours of television a day. That is thirty-five hours a week. If you have a television in your home, put it where it is not so accessible. Take a block of time and say, "I am going to give that time to the Lord." Get some gospel tracts and say, "During the three hours I have been devoting to lesser things, I am going to spend time knocking on doors and speaking to people about Christ."

Are we content to come to church and participate in the services? Are we content just to hang around the temple like these religious leaders? This is what the Lord Jesus was talking about. God's work is an urgent work.

# A UNIQUE WORK

The Bible says in verse twenty-eight, *"Son, go work to day in my vineyard."* This is a unique work.

The word *unique* means "one of a kind." We overuse the word, but this is really what it means. God's work is a unique work. He said, "This is My vineyard." Are we really giving our time to the work of the Lord? Where does God do His work? He does it in the hearts of individuals, but

He also does it in the local church. God is doing His work through His church.

Many fine people have their own agendas, do their own thing, and are as busy as they can be. They call it God's work, but they do nothing in their local church. If it is a unique work, and it is done through the local church, then find out what is going on in your local church and put your heart into it. We do not need to run our own show. We do not need our own projects. If we love the Lord and love the church, then we should get involved in this unique work. We must do God's work God's way through a local, Bible-believing, Bible-preaching church.

*May such an urgency come upon us that we will stop things of lesser importance and start giving time to things of most importance.*

When I was a young man starting out, I sought my pastor for something to do. I said, "Brother Hagan, I must have something to do for the Lord. I want to do something in the church for the Lord." Of course, he let me do some things. These things may have seemed small to some, but they were great to me because they were the Lord's work in the local church.

The Lord's work is a unique work. I thank God that when I trusted Jesus Christ as my Savior, God gave me the promise that when I leave this world I am going to heaven. I also desire to go through life believing that I have found something to do with my life that is going to count for eternity. This is what happens when we begin serving God with other people in the local church.

You may say, "I do not know what to do." If you hunger and thirst after the Lord, you will find something to do. If you want to work for Him, you can work for Him. There is no doubt about it. The Bible says, *"Go work to day in my vineyard."* Get involved in this

*Chapter Twelve*

# THE WICKED HUSBANDMEN

n Matthew, chapter twenty-one, we find our Lord Jesus on His way to Calvary to bleed and die for our sins. It would not be many days until He would die on the cross and pay the sin debt of the whole world, tasting death for every man. He would be taken down by tender, loving hands, buried in a borrowed tomb, and on the third day He would come forth from the grave alive forevermore.

In this passage, Christ came face to face with His bitter enemies. It was as though they were saying, "Where are You from, and who gave You the authority to speak for God? We certainly didn't."

The Lord began speaking to them in parables. We come to one of these parables in Matthew 21:33-46. The Bible says,

> *Hear another parable: There was a certain householder, which planted a vineyard, and hedged*

157

*it round about, and digged a winepress in it, and built a tower, and let it out to husbandmen, and went into a far country: and when the time of the fruit drew near, he sent his servants to the husbandmen, that they might receive the fruits of it. And the husbandmen took his servants, and beat one, and killed another, and stoned another. Again, he sent other servants more than the first: and they did unto them likewise. But last of all he sent unto them his son, saying, They will reverence my son. But when the husbandmen saw the son, they said among themselves, This is the heir; come, let us kill him, and let us seize on his inheritance. And they caught him, and cast him out of the vineyard, and slew him. When the lord therefore of the vineyard cometh, what will he do unto those husbandmen? They say unto him, He will miserably destroy those wicked men, and will let out his vineyard unto other husbandmen, which shall render him the fruits in their seasons. Jesus saith unto them, Did ye never read in the scriptures, The stone which the builders rejected, the same is become the head of the corner: this is the Lord's doing, and it is marvelous in our eyes? Therefore say I unto you, The kingdom of God shall be taken from you, and given to a nation bringing forth the fruits thereof. And whosoever shall fall on this stone shall be broken: but on whomsoever it shall fall, it will grind him to powder. And when the chief priests and Pharisees had heard his parables, they perceived that he spake of them. But when they sought to lay hands on him, they feared the multitude, because they took him for a prophet.*

Notice the expression given to us in the thirty-seventh verse, right in the heart of this parable. The Lord Jesus knew He was delivering words that pierced deeply into their hearts. He said to them, *"But last of all he sent unto them his son."*

This reminds us of the precious verse that says, *"For God so loved the world, that he gave his only begotten Son, that whosoever believeth in him should not perish, but have everlasting life"* (John 3:16).

God sent His Son. If you could imagine meeting your most bitter enemy and telling that person the thing he hated to hear most, this is exactly what Jesus Christ was doing in the face of His enemies. Only a few days before He died, He faced those who so vehemently opposed Him, and those who questioned His authority. In this parable, He told them of the work of God.

There is a parallel account of this parable in the Gospel according to Mark. The Bible says in Mark 12:3-8, speaking of how the husbandmen treated the servants,

> *And they caught him, and beat him, and sent him away empty. And again he sent unto them another servant; and at him they cast stones, and wounded him in the head, and sent him away shamefully handled. And again he sent another; and him they killed, and many others; beating some, and killing some. Having yet therefore one son, his wellbeloved, he sent him also last unto them, saying, They will reverence my son. But those husbandmen said among themselves, This is the heir; come, let us kill him, and the inheritance shall be ours. And they took him, and killed him, and cast him out of the vineyard.*

In this part of the parable, Jesus Christ was speaking of Himself. In this particular parable, we have a greater expression of the love of God than in any other parable the Lord gave. Even the parable of the prodigal son does not express the love of God as does this parable, because God worked patiently with these wicked husbandmen.

Again and again He sent His servants until finally He sent His own Son, and they took Him and killed Him.

For all of us living on this side of the cross, we have no problem understanding what is in the heart of this parable and what Jesus Christ told these wicked religious leaders.

## A PARABLE ABOUT PLANTING

The Bible says in Matthew 21:33, *"Hear another parable: There was a certain householder, which planted a vineyard, and hedged it round about, and digged a winepress in it, and built a tower, and let it out to husbandmen, and went into a far country."*

The Lord Jesus spoke here to the Pharisees. He told them a story about a man who got a certain piece of ground and planted a vineyard. He not only planted a vineyard, but this certain householder hedged it round about. He not only hedged it round about, but he dug a winepress. He made a place in the earth and paved it with stones in order for the juice to drain into a vat. He built a tower which served as a place to watch for enemies and a place of safety for the keeper. He then left the husbandmen to care for the vineyard and went into a far country. His only desire was fruit from this vineyard he had planted.

The planter, or the householder in this parable, is none other than God the Father. This vineyard that He planted is the nation of Israel. However, the vineyard also extends beyond the nation of Israel to the Gentiles, to whom God gave His work when the Jews were set aside because of their rejection of Christ.

The point of this part of the parable is that God put forth all this effort to provide everything that was necessary so there could be fruit from this vineyard. The Lord did it all. He planted it. He built a wall around it. He made the winepress. He built the tower, and He turned the entire vineyard over to husbandmen, or people to work the vineyard. This is exactly what God has done with His kingdom's work in this world.

As we think of God planting this garden, go back to the story of Abraham. He was called of God from Ur of the Chaldees. Think of the promise and covenant that God made with Abraham. This covenant is called the Abrahamic covenant. In this covenant God promised to bless Abraham and to make his seed as the stars of the heaven and the sand of the sea. God raised up from the bosom of Abraham the mighty nation of Israel. Follow Abraham to Isaac, and Isaac to Jacob, and the twelve sons of Jacob down into Egyptian bondage. The mighty nation of Israel was formed in the furnace of Egyptian bondage. Witness them coming out into the wilderness led by Moses and then by Joshua, across the Jordan into the Promised Land.

As an old man, Joshua stood before the children of Israel in the Promised Land making his "farewell address." This address is found in Joshua, chapter twenty-four. In Joshua's speech he made reference to what the Lord had done in order to have fruit in His vineyard. The account of Joshua's address is given in Joshua 24:1-15,

> And Joshua gathered all the tribes of Israel to Shechem, and called for the elders of Israel, and for their heads, and for their judges, and for their officers; and they presented themselves before God. And Joshua said unto all the people, Thus saith the LORD God of Israel, Your fathers dwelt on the other side of the flood in old time, even Terah, the father of Abraham, and the father of Nachor: and they served other gods. And I took your father Abraham from the other side of the flood, and led him throughout all the land of Canaan, and multiplied his seed, and gave him Isaac. And I gave unto Isaac Jacob and Esau: and I gave unto Esau mount Seir, to possess it; but Jacob and his children went down into Egypt. I sent

*Moses also and Aaron, and I plagued Egypt, according to that which I did among them: and afterward I brought you out. And I brought your fathers out of Egypt: and ye came unto the sea; and the Egyptians pursued after your fathers with chariots and horsemen unto the Red sea. And when they cried unto the LORD, he put darkness between you and the Egyptians, and brought the sea upon them, and covered them; and your eyes have seen what I have done in Egypt: and ye dwelt in the wilderness a long season. And I brought you into the land of the Amorites, which dwelt on the other side Jordan; and they fought with you: and I gave them into your hand, that ye might possess their land; and I destroyed them from before you. Then Balak the son of Zippor, king of Moab, arose and warred against Israel, and sent and called Balaam the son of Beor to curse you: but I would not hearken unto Balaam; therefore he blessed you still: so I delivered you out of his hand. And ye went over Jordan, and came unto Jericho: and the men of Jericho fought against you, the Amorites, and the Perizzites, and the Canaanites, and the Hittites, and the Girgashites, the Hivites, and the Jebusites; and I delivered them into your hand. And I sent the hornet before you, which drave them out from before you, even the two kings of the Amorites; but not with thy sword, nor with thy bow. And I have given you a land for which ye did not labour, and cities which ye built not, and ye dwell in them; of the vineyards and oliveyards which ye planted not do ye eat. Now therefore fear the LORD, and serve him in sincerity and in truth: and put away the gods which your fathers served on the other side of the flood, and in Egypt; and serve ye the LORD.*

*And if it seem evil unto you to serve the LORD, choose you this day whom ye will serve; whether the gods which your fathers served that were on the other side of the flood, or the gods of the Amorites, in whose land ye dwell: but as for me and my house, we will serve the LORD.*

Notice carefully what God's Word says in verse thirteen, *"I have given you a land for which ye did not labour, and cities which ye built not, and ye dwell in them; of the vineyards and oliveyards which ye planted not do ye eat."*

The parable in Matthew twenty-one is about planting. God incarnate, the Son of God–co-equal, co-existent with God the Father, and God the Holy Spirit–stood before those men and declared this story. He said to them, "God the Father made a vineyard. He planted it. He put a wall around it. He put the vines in it. He prepared the winepress. He built a tower. He did it all. He planted it, and He gave it to you. All He wants is fruit from the vineyard. All He wants is for you to work in the vineyard. God established it. You come in to be a part of what God has already established."

He spoke primarily to those Jews about what they had been given from the Lord. He spoke of how God had planted for them, and they were the husbandmen. They were to care for God's vineyard, to be the leaders, to be true and loyal to the Lord and His work.

*The point of this part of the parable is that God put forth all this effort to provide everything that was necessary so there could be fruit from this vineyard.*

Let us move past the first century and come to the moment in which we live. We need to think about what God has planted for us to enjoy. Every one of us is a beneficiary of so much that God has already given. We seem to have forgotten just how blessed we are. We seem to have forgotten that our work is not to criticize and fight with one another. Our work is a fruit-bearing work. The Lord of the harvest wants us in the vineyard to bring forth fruit. He wants souls to be won to Christ. He wants us to stay true to the work of the Lord through the centuries. This is a parable about planting.

# A PARABLE ABOUT PRIVILEGE

As the Lord Jesus stood before the Jews that day, He was speaking to the most privileged people on the face of the earth. God had given everything necessary for the fruit to be harvested. The Bible says in Matthew 21:34-39,

> *And when the time of the fruit drew near, he sent his servants to the husbandmen, that they might receive the fruits of it. And the husbandmen took his servants, and beat one, and killed another, and stoned another. Again, he sent other servants more than the first: and they did unto them likewise. But last of all he sent unto them his son, saying, They will reverence my son. But when the husbandmen saw the son, they said among themselves, This is the heir; come, let us kill him, and let us seize on his inheritance. And they caught him, and cast him out of the vineyard, and slew him.*

They were sinning against this privilege. Jesus Christ spoke to these religious leaders, and He said, "Look what the householder has done for you. He sent His servants to gather the fruit." He spoke about the prophets and preachers whom the Lord sent to them.

However, instead of welcoming them and having fruit to place in their hands, the Bible says that these husbandmen became intensified in their evil. They grew worse and worse in their treatment of the servants. First they beat them; then they killed them. But killing them was not enough–they brutally stoned them. Then last of all, God sent His Son. We would think that they would treat the Son wonderfully, but they killed Him.

This is a parable about privilege. No people in all the world were so privileged, but they sinned against their privilege. Today no one in this world is as privileged as those of us in America. Our sin is so great because we sin against such great privilege.

The Bible says in Hebrews 1:1-2, *"God, who at sundry times and in divers manners spake in time past unto the fathers by the prophets, hath in these last days spoken unto us by his Son, whom he hath appointed heir of all things, by whom also he made the worlds."*

In other words, God sent His prophets, but then God sent His Son. This is exactly what the Lord has done. In the closing part of the "hall of faith" the Bible says,

> *And what shall I more say? for the time would fail me to tell of Gedeon, and of Barak, and of Samson, and of Jephthae; of David also, and Samuel, and of the prophets: who through faith subdued kingdoms, wrought righteousness, obtained promises, stopped the mouths of lions, quenched the violence of fire, escaped the edge of the sword, out of weakness were made strong, waxed valiant in fight, turned to flight the armies of the aliens. Women received their dead raised to life again: and others were tortured, not accepting deliverance; that they might obtain a better resurrection: and others had trial of cruel mockings and scourgings, yea, moreover of bonds and imprisonment: they were stoned, they were sawn asunder, were tempted, were slain with the sword: they wandered about in sheepskins and goatskins; being destitute, afflicted, tormented; (Of whom the world was*

*not worthy:) they wandered in deserts, and in mountains, and in dens and caves of the earth* (Hebrews 11:32-38).

What did these Pharisees do with God's servants? What did they do to John the Baptist when he came preaching the Word of God? They cut off his noble head.

Among nations today there is no nation so privileged as our nation. There are no people on the earth so privileged as the people of this mighty nation. But with every passing day there is an increasing disregard toward the things of God and the fundamental truths of the Bible.

> *The Lord of the harvest wants us in the vineyard to bring forth fruit. He wants souls to be won to Christ. He wants us to stay true to the work of the Lord through the centuries.*

We have been handed wonderful privileges. We are recipients of a truly great heritage. Let us not sin against it. We need to continue it and realize that God's servants have always been evil spoken of. God's prophets have always been persecuted. If the Lord Jesus does not come soon, we are going to see things in this nation that we never thought would happen.

I have wondered what would happen if our Savior came to our country today. He would still be taken by vile, wicked hands and put to death because men love darkness rather than light.

In Romans 5:10 the Bible says, *"For if, when we were enemies, we were reconciled to God by the death of his Son, much more, being reconciled, we shall be saved by his life."*

Notice the expression in the first part of verse ten. He says, *"We were enemies."* Every man in his natural state is an enemy of God. We enjoy talking about being reconciled to God by the death of His

Son. We should speak about this and preach the glorious gospel of Christ–His death, burial, and resurrection. However, this gospel is not so glorious until we first realize that we are enemies of God. There is a natural animosity and a vengeance against God and the things of God on the part of unbelievers. We must realize that there is no Good News until we know the bad news, that we are enemies against God. Men love darkness rather than light and position themselves against God and against His dear Son. When we see ourselves as wicked, vile, hell-deserving sinners, then we get a glimpse of how wonderful it is that Jesus Christ was willing to bleed and die for our sins and pay our sin debt.

In my mind I see our Lord standing in close proximity to these people. He was not standing off shouting out these things. This was the Son of God standing face to face with His bitter foes and declaring to them that they were people of great privilege and that they had sinned against that privilege.

Often I think about what God has done for me and how so many others wander in darkness and never hear the truth. I thank God every day that someone cared enough about me to tell me about the Lord Jesus. I thank God that I was led into a Bible-believing, Bible-preaching church. Think of how many people have put their faith in Christ but have never been privileged to be in a strong Bible-believing church that is full of compassion. Many others wander aimlessly through life and die without Christ. We are a privileged people, and we must not sin against that privilege.

## A PARABLE ABOUT PUNISHMENT

The Bible says that, after the husbandmen caught the son, they killed him, and cast him out of the vineyard. This horrible event tells the beautiful story of what Jesus Christ was willing to do for us. In Matthew 21:40 Christ asked the religious leaders, *"When the lord therefore of the vineyard cometh, what will he do unto those husbandmen?"*

In answering the Lord, they condemned themselves. Matthew 21:41-42 says,

> *They say unto him, He will miserably destroy those wicked men, and will let out his vineyard unto other husbandmen, which shall render him the fruits in their seasons. Jesus saith unto them, Did ye never read in the scriptures, The stone which the builders rejected, the same is become the head of the corner: this is the Lord's doing, and it is marvellous in our eyes?*

There are two passages, one in Psalm 118, and one in Daniel 2, about this stone. This stone is Jesus Christ. These leaders were familiar with those Old Testament passages. The Lord taught that He would be rejected, go to Calvary, be spat upon, mocked, and nailed to a cross; but the same One who was rejected was going to become the head of the corner. The Bible prophesied that this is marvelous in our eyes. The Bible says in Matthew 21:43-46,

> *Therefore say I unto you, The kingdom of God shall be taken from you, and given to a nation bringing forth the fruits thereof. And whosoever shall fall on this stone shall be broken: but on whomsoever it shall fall, it will grind him to powder. And when the chief priests and Pharisees had heard his parables, they perceived that he spake of them. But when they sought to lay hands on him, they feared the multitude, because they took him for a prophet.*

Remember that He was looking them directly in the face. He said, "God planted a vineyard. He gave it to you to do His work, to gather fruit for Him. God gave you such a privilege. You have miserably sinned against this privilege, and God is going to take it from you and give it to another."

We are talking about the Jew. We are talking about privilege and sinning against that privilege. The Jews rejected Christ. They had the opportunity to either build on this stone or be crushed by it. Christ offered Himself to the Jews. *"He came unto his own, and his own received him not"* (John 1:11).

After the Jews rejected Christ, there came a time when the work of God was placed into the hands of the Gentiles. The Jews, for a period of time, have been set aside. This is what Jesus Christ speaks of in verse forty-one of this parable.

As we consider that this is a parable about punishment, you may say, "But I am a Christian. I can't die and go to hell. I am saved forever." This is true, but is there no judgment for those who sin against great privilege? What about sinning against the great privilege God has given us, taking it for granted, ceasing to be thankful and grateful to God, ceasing to rejoice over what God has done? The Lord can remove His blessing and leave us to live out the rest of our lives simply going through the mechanical motions of Christianity without His blessing and honor. I have seen it happen to individuals, and I have seen it happen to churches.

*We have been handed wonderful privileges. We are recipients of a truly great heritage. Let us not sin against it.*

If I so desired I could put you into my car and drive you all across this country and show you one place after the other where people were once blessed of God, where He planted something wonderful. They were very privileged, but now they are dry and dead. It is as though they are doomed to live out the rest of their lives and die just going through the motions of what used to be.

We can bring this parable right down to where we live. God has been very good to us. It is so easy to get used to the blessing and take for granted the privilege that God has given us. When we do, God will lift His hand and say, "I want you to know what it is like to live without blessing."

I do not want to live without the blessing of God. This is a parable about planting, about privilege, and about punishment. If we do not want to live without God's blessing, we must never get over the fact that He sent His Son. We must never get over the fact that the Lord Jesus bled and died for our sins, was buried, and rose from the dead. Thank God for the wonderful privilege of knowing Him.

# The Wicked Husbandmen

# THE MARRIAGE OF THE KING'S SON

he Bridegroom is at the door, and He is about to come for His bride. It seems that everyone is eager to know about the Second Coming of Christ. The Lord's coming is at hand. It is purifying to think of the doctrine of the coming of Christ and to love His appearing.

The Lord Jesus said to His disciples in John 14:1-3,

> Let not your heart be troubled: ye believe in God, believe also in me. In my Father's house are many mansions: if it were not so, I would have told you. I go to prepare a place for you. And if I go and prepare a place for you, I will come again, and receive you unto myself; that where I am, there ye may be also.

If this promise was all we had, it would be enough. He said, *"I will come again."* There are over three hundred references in the twenty-seven books of the New Testament to the coming of Christ. Imagine going down a road twenty-seven miles long with three hundred signs declaring, "The King is coming! The King is coming! The King is coming!" By the time you reached the end of the road, you would believe that the King is coming. As we read the Bible, we get the message that the King is coming.

Our Lord revealed His thoughts to the religious leaders of His day. He met them face to face and spoke to them in a way that no man had ever spoken to them. We find a parable given to us in Matthew 22:1-14,

> *And Jesus answered and spake unto them again by parables, and said, The kingdom of heaven is like unto a certain king, which made a marriage for his son, and sent forth his servants to call them that were bidden to the wedding: and they would not come. Again, he sent forth other servants, saying, Tell them which are bidden, Behold, I have prepared my dinner: my oxen and my fatlings are killed, and all things are ready: come unto the marriage. But they made light of it, and went their ways, one to his farm, another to his merchandise: and the remnant took his servants, and entreated them spitefully, and slew them. But when the king heard thereof, he was wroth: and he sent forth his armies, and destroyed those murderers, and burned up their city. Then saith he to his servants, The wedding is ready, but they which were bidden were not worthy. Go ye therefore into the highways, and as many as ye shall find, bid to the marriage. So those servants went out into the highways, and gathered together all as many as they found, both bad and good: and the wedding was furnished with guests. And when the king came in to see the guests, he saw there a man which had not on a wedding garment: and he saith unto him, Friend,*

*how camest thou in hither not having a wedding garment? And he was speechless. Then said the king to the servants, Bind him hand and foot, and take him away, and cast him into outer darkness; there shall be weeping and gnashing of teeth. For many are called, but few are chosen.*

The Lord said, *"The wedding is ready."* This is a wonderful parable. This parabolic teaching starts back in Matthew chapter twenty-one. The Bible says in Matthew 21:23-27,

*And when he was come into the temple, the chief priests and the elders of the people came unto him as he was teaching, and said, By what authority doest thou these things? and who gave thee this authority? And Jesus answered and said unto them, I also will ask you one thing, which if ye tell me, I in like wise will tell you by what authority I do these things. The baptism of John, whence was it? from heaven, or of men? And they reasoned within themselves, saying, If we shall say, From heaven; he will say unto us, Why did ye not then believe him? But if we shall say, Of men; we fear the people; for all hold John as a prophet. And they answered Jesus, and said, We cannot tell. And he said unto them, Neither tell I you by what authority I do these things.*

In verse twenty-eight He began a parable. In verse thirty-three, He said, *"Hear another parable."* In verse one of chapter twenty-two, He gave another parable. When He finished these parables, they thought they would trick Him. In Matthew 22:16 the Bible says that they sent the Herodians, and the Lord Jesus silenced them. In verse twenty-three, they sent the Sadducees, and He silenced them. Then in verse thirty-five they sent one of the Pharisees, who was a lawyer, and Christ silenced him. Finally, the Bible says in verse forty-six,

*"And no man was able to answer him a word, neither durst any man from that day forth ask him any more questions."*

# THE INTERPRETATION OF THE PARABLE

This parable is rather easy to interpret. The Bible says in Matthew 22:1-3, *"And Jesus answered and spake unto them again by parables, and said, The kingdom of heaven is like unto a certain king, which made a marriage for his son, and sent forth his servants to call them that were bidden to the wedding: and they would not come."*

*The Lord's coming is at hand. It is purifying to think of the doctrine of the coming of Christ.*

What does all this mean? The king in this parable is God the Father. The son is none other than the Lord Jesus Christ. The servants are His preachers of the gospel. We find in this parable that the servants go out and bid the guests to come to a wedding feast. There is going to be a marriage supper. The Bible says that when these guests were bidden to come, it was not that they could not come, but the Bible says in verse three, that *"they would not come."*

The Son of God came from heaven's glory and bled and died on Calvary's cross. He suffered our death for us. He tasted death for every man. He purchased salvation full, free, and forever for anyone who would trust Him. He bids all the world, *"Come unto me, all ye that labour and are heavy laden, and I will give you rest"* (Matthew 11:28).

The Bible says, *"For God so loved the world, that he gave his only begotten Son, that whosoever believeth in him should not perish, but have everlasting life"* (John 3:16).

All men can come to Him for salvation. It is not that these in the parable could not come. They made a decision that they would not come.

Think of how many people we know who have been bidden to come, but will not come. I thank God I have accepted the invitation, and I am going to the marriage supper.

In Revelation 19:7 the Bible says, *"Let us be glad and rejoice, and give honour to him: for the marriage of the Lamb is come, and his wife hath made herself ready."*

In this marriage, the Lord Jesus is our heavenly Bridegroom. The church is the bride. Verse eight says, *"And to her was granted that she should be arrayed in fine linen, clean and white: for the fine linen is the righteousness of saints."*

They are clothed in righteousness–not their own, but His. At the end of chapter three of the Revelation of Jesus Christ, the church disappears. We do not see the church again until we come to the nineteenth chapter. The Bible says in Revelation 19:9-16,

> *And he saith unto me, Write, Blessed are they which are called unto the marriage supper of the Lamb. And he saith unto me, These are the true sayings of God. And I fell at his feet to worship him. And he said unto me, See thou do it not: I am thy fellowservant, and of thy brethren that have the testimony of Jesus: worship God: for the testimony of Jesus is the spirit of prophecy. And I saw heaven opened, and behold a white horse; and he that sat upon him was called Faithful and True, and in righteousness he doth judge and make war. His eyes were as a flame of fire, and on his head were many crowns; and he had a name written, that no man knew, but he himself. And he was clothed with a vesture dipped in blood: and his name is called The Word of God. And the armies which were*

> *in heaven followed him upon white horses, clothed in fine linen, white and clean. And out of his mouth goeth a sharp sword, that with it he should smite the nations: and he shall rule them with a rod of iron: and he treadeth the winepress of the fierceness and wrath of Almighty God. And he hath on his vesture and on his thigh a name written, KING OF KINGS, AND LORD OF LORDS.*

In verse nine, we see the marriage supper of the Lamb. However, there is another supper. The Bible says in verse seventeen, *"And I saw an angel standing in the sun; and he cried with a loud voice, saying to all the fowls that fly in the midst of heaven, Come and gather yourselves together unto the supper of the great God..."*

There is going to be a slaying of people. We can either come to the marriage supper of the Lamb or perish in this supper of the great God. The Bible continues in verses eighteen through twenty,

> *...that ye may eat the flesh of kings, and the flesh of captains, and the flesh of mighty men, and the flesh of horses, and of them that sit on them, and the flesh of all men, both free and bond, both small and great. And I saw the beast, and the kings of the earth, and their armies, gathered together to make war against him that sat on the horse, and against his army. And the beast was taken, and with him the false prophet that wrought miracles before him, with which he deceived them that had received the mark of the beast, and them that worshipped his image. These both were cast alive into a lake of fire burning with brimstone.*

This speaks of the Antichrist and the False Prophet. I do not know everything they are going to do during the Tribulation, but I know that when the Tribulation is over, and the Son of God comes in glory, they are going to be taken and cast into a lake of fire and brimstone without being able to lift a finger against God's Son.

In the parable in Matthew twenty-two, our Lord was talking about those who were bidden to come and trust Him as Savior and believe on Him. God the Father has sent God the Son, and we can come to God the Son as the Holy Spirit comes to draw us through His servants who are preaching His Word. If we will not come to the marriage supper, then we can expect to be a part of the supper of the great God. When we compare Scripture with Scripture, it is very clear what this parable means.

## THE INVITATION IN THIS PARABLE

In Matthew 22:8-9 the Bible says, *"Then saith he to his servants, The wedding is ready, but they which were bidden were not worthy. Go ye therefore into the highways, and as many as ye shall find, bid to the marriage."*

As He gave this message, our Lord was standing face to face with Jewish leaders. He had invited them to come, but they would not come.

The Bible says in John 1:11-12, *"He came unto his own, and his own received him not. But as many as received him, to them gave he power to become the sons of God, even to them that believe on his name."*

This is His invitation. If there is no invitation, Christ died in vain. He suffered the agonies of hell on the cross of Calvary. He bled and died. He was separated from God. Did He shed His precious blood for naught? If there is no invitation, He died in vain.

God does not leave us lingering with the thought of those who will not come to Him, but He tells us of those who did come. Have you accepted His royal invitation? The Bible says in Matthew 22:10, *"So those servants went out into the highways, and gathered together all as many as they found, both bad and good: and the wedding was furnished with guests."*

Everyone we think might come may not come, but we can thank God that there are those who will come. God chooses to use the base things. God's Word says in I Corinthians 1:28, *"And base things of the world, and things which are despised, hath God chosen, yea, and things which are not, to bring to nought things that are."*

I love reading about the life and ministry of Charles Spurgeon. Recently, I found something in my reading that I had never found before. I learned that most of the people in the Metropolitan Tabernacle were poor people from London. Spurgeon went into the highways and hedges of London and reached the poor, the overlooked, and the neglected. God blessed Spurgeon for going after them. He went after them and they came.

Can you imagine how these people in this parable felt when they came? They had never dined at a king's table. They had never been bidden to come to a place like this before. They had never been treated royally. They were the outcasts, the forgotten, the overlooked, the trampled down in life. The king said, "Come to my table."

I thank God that He knocked at my heart's door and said, "Come to the King's table." We need to thank God that we are children of the King. I am reminded of the song that says,

> My Father is rich in houses and lands.
> He holdeth the wealth of the world in His hands.
> Of rubies and diamonds, of silver and gold,
> His coffers are full, He has riches untold.
> I'm a child of the King, a child of the King.
> With Jesus my Savior, I'm a child of the King.

There is a wonderful invitation in this parable. Have you accepted His invitation?

# THE INTRUDER IN THIS PARABLE

The Bible says in verse eleven, *"And when the king came in to see the guests, he saw there a man which had not on a wedding garment."*

This man was not prepared for the wedding. There is an interesting thing to notice here. Many made light of the invitation and would not come, but here is one who made light of it and did come. This causes us to think seriously about the matter of our salvation. Do you know that you are saved?

What is this wedding garment? I have no righteousness of my own. I have no merit of my own, but I thank God that I have a wedding garment. It was given to me by the Son of God. The Bible says in Isaiah 61:10,

> *I will greatly rejoice in the Lord, my soul shall be joyful in my God; for he hath clothed me with the garments of salvation, he hath covered me with the robe of righteousness, as a bridegroom decketh himself with ornaments, and as a bride adorneth herself with her jewels.*

My garment is the robe of righteousness. It is not my own, but Jesus Christ's. I have no righteousness of my own. The Bible says that *"all our righteousnesses are as filthy rags"* (Isaiah 64:6). The words *"filthy rags"* have to do with rags wrapped around a pus-filled sore on a leper's body. The filthy rags would be soaked with the pus. The Holy Spirit of God says that our righteousnesses are as those filthy rags.

We have nothing good to present to God. If we think for one moment that we have done anything that can bring us to God, then we must realize that we are no better than Cain who brought the firstfruits of his own harvest and said, "Lord, this is the way I am coming." God had made it plain that the only way he could come was the blood way. The only way to God is by the blood of Christ. There is no other way to God.

Does it break your heart to think about how many people in so many churches are saying that they have done something to get to heaven? They think they have earned their way to glory, but they are going to die lost. They will go to hell forever because they do not have the wedding garment of the righteousness of Jesus Christ.

*My garment is the robe of righteousness. It is not my own, but His. I have no righteousness of my own.*

This man was not a guest; he was an intruder. The king came in, and he saw that this man had no wedding garment. God sees everything. No matter how well we may pretend, He sees into our soul. He sees if we are covered in the blood of Jesus Christ.

Are you washed in the soul-cleansing blood of the Lamb? This is the only garment that will get you in. The Bible says in verses eleven and twelve, *"And when the king came in to see the guests, he saw there a man which had not on a wedding garment: and he saith unto him, Friend, how camest thou in hither not having a wedding garment? And he was speechless."*

Let me ask you this question, "When you die and stand before God and meet the Lord, what will you say to God about why He should let you into His heaven?" There can only be one of three responses to this question. Some might say, "Lord, You should let me in because of what I have done." Maybe they have reformed, tried hard, or simply believed in the existence of God. They believe that something they have done will get them to heaven, but it never will. There is no saving power in baptism. There is no salvation in taking some ordinance of the church. There is no salvation in attending church. There is no salvation in singing the songs, preaching the sermons, or teaching the classes. There is no salvation in simply being born into a Christian home. There will be people who think that because they have done something, they will get to heaven. We do not get to heaven because of something good we have done.

The second response to this question is to say nothing. Some will have no answer. They will be speechless like this man in the parable. They will not get to heaven.

The third response will be given by those who will say, "I am trusting the Lord Jesus." I do not want anyone to be confused about salvation. We are not saved through some formula. People say to me sometimes, "I did not pray the right prayer." What is the right prayer? There is no right prayer. It is simply believing God. A man who cannot speak can get saved by his faith in God from his heart.

When did you get saved? You may say, "I got saved in church." Where did you get saved in church? Did you get saved at the altar? Did you get saved at your seat? Did you get saved somewhere between your seat and the altar? Where did you get saved? You got saved the moment you asked God to forgive your sin and you put your faith in Christ for salvation. Salvation is instant and complete the moment we trust the Lord Jesus.

In this parable, we see a man who took the invitation lightly and came. There were others who took it lightly and did not come. They found every excuse not to come. This unprepared guest was not serious about coming. There are people who are numbered among God's people who are not serious about coming, who do not have the wedding garment. They are intruders. They really do not belong in God's family. They could become a part if they would. The invitation has gone out. The wedding is ready. Our heavenly Bridegroom is coming for His own.

Sunday School materials are available for use in conjunction with *The Parables of Jesus*. For a complete listing of available materials from Crown Publications, please call 1-877 AT CROWN or write to: P.O. Box 159 ❖ Powell, TN ❖ 37849

Visit us on the Web at
www.FaithfortheFamily.com
*"A Website for the Christian Family"*

# ABOUT THE AUTHOR

Clarence Sexton is the pastor of the Temple Baptist Church and founder of Crown College in Knoxville, Tennessee. He has written more than twenty books and booklets. He speaks in conferences throughout the United States and has conducted training sessions for pastors and Christian workers in several countries around the world. He and his wife, Evelyn, have been married for thirty-five years. They have two grown sons and six grandchildren. For more information about the ministry of Clarence Sexton, visit our website at www.FaithfortheFamily.com.

## OTHER HELPFUL BOOKS BY CLARENCE SEXTON:

THE LORD IS MY SHEPHERD

EARNESTLY CONTEND FOR THE FAITH

THE CHRISTIAN HOME

TRUTHS EVERY CHRISTIAN NEEDS TO KNOW

LORD, SEND A REVIVAL

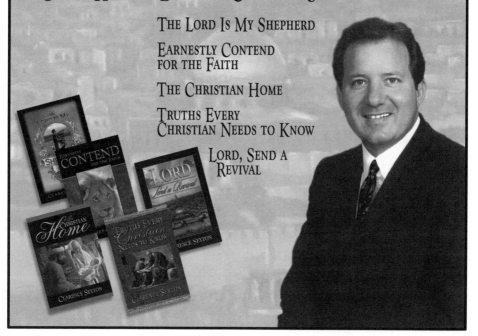

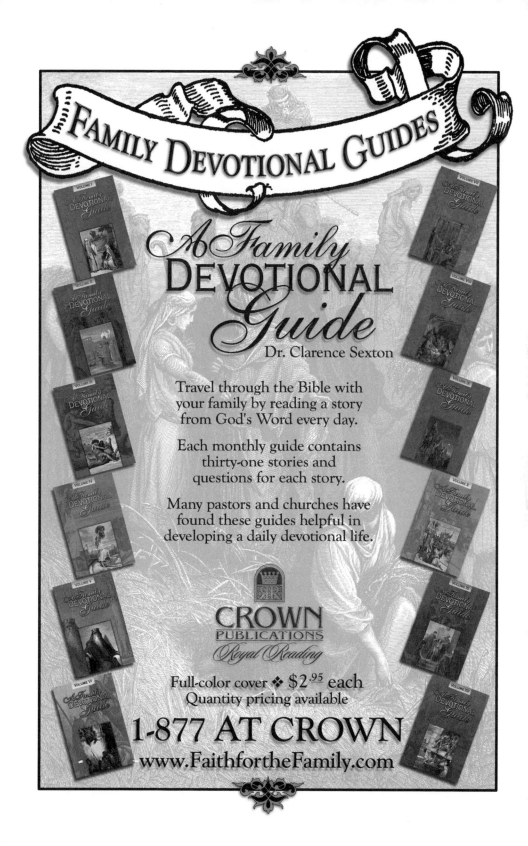